She Loves Me,

She Loves Me Not

365 Poems to Lift You Up, Crush Your Soul, and Lift You Back Up Again

by

Autumn Siders

Copyright © 2021 by Autumn B. Siders
All rights reserved. This book or any portion thereof
may not be reproduced or used in any manner whatsoever
without the express written permission of the publisher
except for the use of brief quotations in a book review.

Printed in the United States of America

First Printing, 2021

ISBN 9781736491904

E.M. Sanchez Press
PO Box 82
Moultonborough, NH 03254

www.autumnsiders.com

Also by Autumn Siders:

#nofilter

Not My Type: Stories

Spermeo & Juliegg: A Reproductive Tragedy

Travels with Clancy: Poetry from Coast to Coast

<u>Children's Books</u>

E.M. Sanchez Mysteries

To the one who loves herself,
and loves me not.

January 1

She Loves Me

She loves me,
She loves me not.
She loves me,
She loves me a lot.
She loves me,
She loves me not at all.
She loves me,
She loves me in the fall.
Falling petals fade.
Fading memories bleed.
Bleeding hearts beat.
Beating the game—I will.
She loves me,
She loves me a lot.

January 2

Little Light

Winter's chill never seemed so warm.
Hell beats up
while my soul remains disarmed.
A blanket sleep of white frozen rain
wraps me up
and masks the ever-present pain.
The only angel around for miles
conjured up
by this empty corpse that still smiles.
The demons have come and gone,
fed up
with what little light lingers on.

January 3

Chartreuse

I've seen golden sunsets
that put the word beauty
to shame.
I've seen pink and purple hues
that warm the heart and soul:
a muse.
I've seen burning reds
that end in a fiery kiss,
and more.
There is but one shade,
I've left to see:
a chartreuse sky,
over you and me.

January 4

Never

When I wrote that song for you,
I never imagined a time
life existed without you
and words refused to rhyme.
When I said those words to you,
I never knew you'd never
say them back,
and from that moment on,
never became
a word
I never knew
you knew
could
hurt.

January 5

Seagull

To be as free as a gull
and enjoy the trash we've been given
would be an enlightened state
to our hearts that act so driven.

The sweet salt air
against our faces, under our wings,
the sky ahead and earth below,
each thermal a new dream brings.

What's so wrong with a life
up in the clouds, high in the sky?
Forget enlightened, and free;
contentment is in a french fry.

January 6

The minor chords hit me hard.
It's not that the majors don't lift,
it's that the minors resonate.
When it cuts to the bone,
the mark never fades.
The music plays on,
the feeling deepens,
hope moves on,
darkness seeps in.
A minor problem,
a major moment,
a note of regret,
an eternal rest.

January 7

The Little Things

I wonder if anyone else,
who doesn't know it's there,
can hear it.
So subtle on the track
we laid that day,
but I love it.
It doesn't matter how many
times I listen,
it always beguiles
to hear not only the words you sing,
but the moment that
your lips smile.

January 8

Mother Nature's Divorce

She's helpless, you know.
How many times has she
tried to kick him out now?
He keeps saying he'll change,
the lying drunk,
the destructive fuck.

"I'll do better,
you'll see.
I'll clean up my act,
I'll plant a tree."

His flowery language,
sure to wilt
by the last breath
of his drastic lilt.

She got mad, sure.
She threw it all at him:
the vase, the heat,
the viral masterpiece.
He dodged left, then right,
and was finally brought to his knees.

His face, a mask, of death,
uttered the words to please.

"I love you, it's true,
I couldn't live without you."

I keep hoping She'll change
because I know without a doubt,
She could be surprised by
what she can live without.

January 9

Silence

Some try to fill it.
Some force it on others.
Loss elicits moments of
and secrets demand it.
Some cannot sleep without it.
Some cannot think without it.
It can be awkward
or it can be comforting.
Tense, notable, reverent.
I've always known it
as peace.

January 10

Treasures

Been searching so long
for that fountain of youth.
Forgettin' to live,
seeking foolish proof.
Atlantis sunk in the sea.
El dorado lost its glimmer.
Drowning in the drink,
those golden years are gettin' slimmer.
Pirates' booty and ancient lands,
marked by "x" on an agèd map,
slipped through crooked fingers,
heading for a dusty dirt nap.

January 11

Home Sweet Kitten

Where cat hair
coats the chair
and toys are scattered
by a gentle patter.
Love is there
in that bitter glare
as long as the bowl
is always full.
A purr and a snore
makes my heart feel more
as I, the foolish creep
watch you dream and sleep.
But, this home sweet home
would feel so alone
without this thief
who stole my heart.

January 12

My Own Device

Any day now, I know it,
the shadows will come
and drag me in a fit
to where it is I belong.

The past will catch me,
it is never far behind.
This heart is so empty,
it won't be long.

This prison of my own device
is a far better Hell
than my impending demise;
it is where I belong.

January 13

Marked

I've used both fists
& words,
and I can honestly say,
both will leave marks
if used the correct way.

January 14

This Time

I've been holding my breath so long,
waiting for the other shoe to drop,
but the lungs can only be deprived
for a short while before they stop.

Gasping, fighting, falling in the depths.
Waiting, hoping, dying in your wake.
Time might heal some wounds,
but this time, can't take away the ache.

January 15

Keep Driving

I miss the road the most.
Blacktop for miles and the stars above.
Headlights, the only beacon
on a cold desert road.
The open window,
my hand fighting the force,
cutting through the wind
that exists only because
I keep moving.

January 16

Happy Quill

The ink ran out,
it would seem the well dried.
Words, that once sparked flame,
flicker out on the tip of my tongue.
O, happy quill,
you once gave life,
now you are sheathed
and left to rust
and die.

January 17

Amber Skies

Aching muscles
and amber skies,
a hard day's work
and sleepy eyes.
The sun sinks low
and daylight dies,
but next to you,
my heart flies.

January 18

Inflation

Pennies in a well
don't get you the same wish
you could have years ago.
Damn inflation.
Chuck a quarter.
maybe you'll get
exactly what you deserve
and not a penny more.

January 19

No Time

You make it sound like forever
is such a long time.
But such a short while
seems like a crime.
Eternity would not do
when it comes to loving you.
Infinite tomorrows
still require time borrowed.
Even if we were granted
all the universe could give,
my love would runneth over
longer than we could live.

January 20

Old Soul

I blame all the folks
who told me I was an old soul.
It's like my body heard
and tried to catch up
at an accelerated rate.

Now, thirty is the new ninety,
aches, pains, grays
are my personal fate.

Was it worth it?

Always being a step ahead.
An agèd soul, a wiser brain.

No, I've got a bone to pick.
Each day, energy drained,
my soul, too, gets sick.

January 21

To Build a Fire

Dusk sets,
flakes float,
and flames rise.
Silence envelops
until a log cracks
and the fire grows in size.
Rosy cheeks,
no longer cold,
but heated by the fire.
Nature's calm
contentment wraps
around a soul so

January 22

tired and fading
the flames simmer down.
The chill encroaches,
a coyote approaches
nighttime
comes alive.
Glowing ember,
heat remembered
like a phantom
on the skin.
Soon the light
will all be gone,
the heat, the flame
allow the cold
to win.

To Lose a Fire

January 23

Listening

Seeing the world from another's eyes
could do the world a lot of good.
It could make a heart grow in size
and break down walls of steel and wood.

Imagine seeing a neighbor
in a completely different light,
putting away the gun and saber
and waging peace, ending the fight.

How many times has anger
resulted in the end of life
when voices become clangor
drowning out another's strife?

Listening could be the answer,
it could even be the cure
to cutting out this cancer
and turning humans pure.

January 24

Race to the End

Pen scratching paper,
racing to finish a thought.
352 left,
but even one feels like a lot.
If you aren't there to read them,
who else could I trust?
These words on a page
will also turn to dust.
Who could ever replace
a reader such as you?
The race to finish is on
and I've got so much to do.

January 25

Drunk

Intoxicated,
but only in your presence.
Always drunk on you.

January 26

Piece of Work

Art is meant to be seen
from afar.
Up close, all the flaws
are exposed.
Every brush stroke,
bared.
Every imperfection,
blatant.
Beauty, heart, and soul
can only be perceived
at a distance.

You,
are a piece of art.

January 27

Good Book

That new book smell
and a cup of tea,
steam floods up,
the plot runs free.
Nothing to do,
nowhere to be,
pages to turn,
places to see.

January 28

Going Down with the Ship

It would be terrible
to die before finishing.
All my characters left
to fend for themselves.

Dangling ends, like nerves,
severed, bloody, painful.
Ideas dead, synapses
no longer firing.

When I die,
so do countless others.

Poor souls,
going down with the ship
was never
supposed to be their fate.

January 29

Acts of Kindness

Riots, shootings,
injustices on every corner.
Cities on fire,
full of mourners.
The cameras are pointed
on every ounce of hate;
let's hope they turn them
before it's too late.
With every deed of bad,
acts of kindness go unseen.
Look into your hearts
and away from the screen.

January 30

Frozen Ink

It's too damn cold,
the ink won't run,
and now declarations,
look faded in the sun.

Surely this is a message,
that life should be penciled in
since it could all dry up,
subject to a whim.

The bitter chill,
will keep me down today,
and winter winds are coming,
almost surely to stay.

January 31

Want v. Need

I think about what I want,
and then I think about what I need;
the two never seem to mesh
and my conscience must concede.

The older that I get,
needs nag at want
and tell my hopeless heart,
"be happy with what you got."

Perhaps this is nirvana,
or a way to remove the sting,
but happiness is achieved
when want & need are the same thing.

February 1

Shitty Coffee

This coffee tastes like shit.
Okay, not shit,
but it's pretty bad.
I'll drink it
since that's how the world
has come to taste.
Contentment with
faults, flaws,
bad customer service,
and shitty coffee.

At least it's hot,
so I can scald
the taste buds on my tongue,
but nothing
can help me stomach
the swill
I've come to expect.

February 2

Oh Deer

It's quite possible
I've spoken to more deer
than humans
at this point.

I see a person
and I'm stuck,
like a deer
in the headlights.

Fight or flight;
it's safer to chose flight,
so I flee
into the night.

I see a deer
and I put the car in park,
I roll down the window
and pour out my heart.

The deer, stares,
in the headlights.
Fight or flight.

She too,
runs into the night.

February 3

Strays

There were about thirty cats,
maybe ten dogs
roaming the plaza,
almost in a fog.
I had rounded the corner,
like they called my name
and my heart broke,
humanity to blame.
Down to my last euros,
I hit el supermercado,
bought some food
for the pups y los gatos.
Broke and broken,
I waited for them to eat,
then I shed some tears
quietly admitting defeat.

February 4

P Makes Me Think of You

Partner,
pal,
the perfect person
to perpetuate
peace, promise, and
positivity.
You purloined
my pessimistic
pertinacity
and provoked
this pusillanimous heart
to a paragon
of playful poise.

Perhaps,
your purpose
is to pioneer
the poetic pacification
of a planet
patiently awaiting
the perfect person
to perpetuate

peace, promise, and
positivity.

February 5

Schrödinger

Wet snow
falls from the roof
offering up a splat
as it hits the ground.
Chill creeps in
and I pull the covers up,
not wanting to leave
the fading warmth of sleep.

No sound, no light,
the house has not
yet risen.

If I decide
myself to rise
and venture to your room,
will I be met with life
or struck with horror?

Best not
open the door.

February 6

G.O.A.T

The goats,
they get me every time.
So clumsy,
so cute,
so cuddly.
I wave,
to the television,
foolishly,
child-like,
hopelessly.
Stoicism,
I wear it,
happily,
casually,
constantly.
But then,
sometimes,
I just think about the goats.

February 7

Bleak

Bleak
is such a beautiful word.

Barren,
charmless,
miserable,
hopeless,
forbidding.

And then,
there's bleak.
A word that capture all that
in one syllable.

February 8

Loner

Families,
not everyone
has got one.
Loners do,
in fact,
exist.
Even harder
to believe,
we actually
like
being
alone.

February 9

My Bad

Sorry doesn't cut it
for some wrongs.
Words fall flat,
yours grow long.

Apologies,
condolences,
my bad.

Fucked over,
stolen land,
disease spread,
battle in hand.

Forgive us,
excuse us,
oops.

Let's fix this,
forget the past;
we tried to erase you,
but it didn't last.

Sorry,
mea culpa,
my bad.

February 10

Ink & Vinyl

    the needle scratches,
    while the needle scratches
impressions,
    images,
        memories,
            melodies,
                poignant,
                    pressed,
                  vinyl,
                      vibrations,
                  voices,
              victories,
            colors,
        chords,
      pain,
promise,
    the needle lifts,
    then the needle lifts

February 11

Lights Out

When the light goes out,

hopefully your eyes have seen

more than just darkness.

February 12

42nd **Poem**

Sweet little child,
I watch you sleep
and I myself dream
about how to keep
you forever.

Sweet perfect soul,
I know in my heart
that you had it stolen
from the very start.
-Yours forever

February 13

All Science Aside

All science aside,
can't you see how clearly
She hides?
Torrential rains,
blizzards,
tsunamis,
flames.

All science aside,
have you not noticed
Her pain?
Polluted oceans,
skies,
stale earth,
no motions.

All science aside,
what will you say when
She has died?
Will you mourn for more
than your resources
that have dried?

February 14

A Moment

Sure,
that breath before the kiss,
gazing into your eyes moment
is great,
but could you imagine
experiencing that all the time?

Dry eyes, palpitations,
and shortness of breath.

Give me a night
on the couch
wrapped in your arms
and that,
is a moment
that can last.

February 15

Signed

The Founding Fathers
must have been so proud,
signing and shouting,
raising a patriotic crowd.

If only they could see
all their hard work today
and know how those patriots
signed humanity away.

February 16

Bare

Waiting downstairs
while you fix your hair,
apply some make-up
and remain unaware
that none of that,
nor what you wear
will change the fact
that I'll always stare
at all the beauty
your soul can bare.

February 17

Kerf

I never heard
"timber"
as my heart fell.
There was no hope
of catching it,
a stump you sliced
so well.

Who knew
I was so attached
to a muscle of inferior worth?
At least I can prove
your guilt
through this bloody, sappy kerf.

February 18

Picture

Worth a thousand words
and still, not a single one,
captures the true meaning
of watching the rising sun.
Still frame, in present time,
with company, or by one's self,
the dawn's arrival
puts yesterday on the shelf.
The colors, the promise
of another chance
provides a beauty
worthy of more than a glance.
Worthy of hope
and hopeful for change,
picture a world
a sunrise can arrange.

February 19

Melt for You

I loved you as you never knew.
The way the waves crash,
the way the winds blow,
the way the storms brew.

I felt you deep into my soul.
The way the trees sway,
the way the leaves blow,
the way the thunder rolls.

I kept you always in my heart.
The way the birds sing,
the way the stars light,
the way the seasons start.

I loved you like the dawn.
And, like a bee, you made it sting,
but soon you faded to winter
as I melted in the spring.

February 20

Casualty

I thought the end
would be more bleak,
not enjoying family
week after week.
Where's all the brimstone,
the fire, the ruin?
It's possible we panicked
just a little too soon.
It's not all sunshine;
there's certainly fear.
But, life's ups and downs
are not always clear.
If the end is nigh,
you could have fooled me
because compassion still
has not fallen casualty.

February 21

Love Poem

Two hearts,
roses,
clichés,
eternity.
No one tells you
after eternity
and empty promises,
and wilted flowers,
you still have
but one heart
and a love poem
that ends.

February 22

Dock of the Bay

Sitting on a dock
of the bay,
a lone soul,
on a cloudy day.
Pencil and journal,
the old-fashioned way.
Private thoughts
become things to say.
This stranger to me
remains this way:
a thoughtful imprint
meant to stay,
sitting on a dock
of the bay.

February 23

Last Call

You don't have to go home,
in fact, you can't.
You can't stay here,
in fact, there is no here left.
While you were nursing that beer,
way in the back,
this place burned down.
Did you even notice the flames,
or are they not the only thing
over your head?

February 24

In Transition

Some things
assigned at birth
hold no merit
nor define our worth.
Pronouns on paper
and drastic decisions,
finding truth
in freeing incisions.
Pain and pride,
shame and salvation,
walking the line
of eternal damnation.
Braver than most
unable to live a lie,
hopeful for a future
with a bluer sky.
Different, yet the same,
and still some are blind
to the fact that a human
exists in that mind.
Hatred and venom,
a misguided position

of fools who don't know
we're all in transition.

February 25

Thundersnow

Wind's picked up again
and this really blows.
Branches whip about
and the snow pile grows.
Forces of nature,
with which you don't fuck,
have decided today
you shall be down on luck.
Let the storm pass
to some other soul,
don't interrupt
thunder on a roll.

.

February 26

Masquerade

Twelve eyes,
at least that's the initial count.
The fire crackles,
near its end,
but apparently this masked ball
is about to begin.
There will be no music or dance,
but enjoy the leftovers
for as long as they last.

February 27

Ever?

Ever looked Evil in the eye?
Or seen darkness in a soul?
Ever been hung out to dry?
Or fallen down a hole?

Ever felt pure despair?
Or felt the need to atone?
Ever had lungs without air?
Or realized you're all alone?

Ever wondered if others
felt the way you do?
Or does the pain of others
mean not a thing to you?

February 28

On Loan

the beat
in your heart
the bass
in my soul
the heat
like a dart
your embrace
that I stole

the love
that we share
the night
that we own
kind of
not fair
to those who fight
for love on loan

Go to page 400 for leap day

March 1

Target Practice

We fired off some rounds,
basic target practice shit.
Paper bulls-eyes, earth mounds,
laughing with every hit.

I never knew back then,
while I was working on my aim,
you let your anger out of the pen
and started finding others to blame.

What could I have done
to make you change your ways?
Living your life by the gun
has put your head into a haze.

March 2

Relief

I saw you walking
after you died,
down the road,
late at night.
Call me crazy,
call it grief;
my heart calls it
pure relief.

March 3

Snowball

The lies roll off your tongue,
smooth as a snake
slithering from sin.
Can you keep track
of what's even true?
Have the lies become fact?
Do they define you?
One becomes two
and two becomes ten.
Each toxic drip
destroys what had been.
The bigger it gets,
that snowball is packed
and poised to harm.
Best hope for your sake,
those lies don't start to warm.

March 4

Bedtime Stories

Finishing the coffee
before it gets cold
takes precedence over
the book I hold.
It's not that the story
holds no intrigue,
but caffeine is needed
to combat fatigue.
The characters, the plot
are deepening on me
to move it along
to whatever may be.
Stories are meant
to move and inspire
the dreams of a slumber
to the tomorrows we acquire.

March 5

479

I kindly stopped for Death,
but He could not stop for me.
I waited for His carriage
to take me to eternity.

No hoofbeats rang
nor horses neighed;
Just silence and I
on my conscience weighed.

He could have called
or sent a sign
to explain why life
is so divine.

So now I'll wait
for my joyous ride
when Death has time
to be my guide.

March 6

I Could

I could sit and watch
as you scream and shout.
I could back away
and let you sort it out.

I could hear those words,
Muslim, illegal, fag, Jew
but pretend they are just words
not to do with me, but with you.

I could go home
and just wait my turn
until your hate becomes murder
and these words boil and churn.

I could wait until
those screams turn to fists
and look on in horror
as blood fiercely mists.

I could do all this
but then am I to blame
when the headline this week
is another soul has been maimed?

I could stand up
and make my voice heard,
stand beside a fellow human
and push back your bitter words.

I could stand up
and you could stand down
and realize that differences
are what make the world go 'round.

I could lecture you on love
but you are just so full of hate,
so instead I'll show you love
and all it can create.

March 7

A Day in the World

Those days,
we were wild and free,
top of the world,
just you and me.

These days,
we are broken and scarred,
marred by the world
that made us both hard.

Innocence lost,
and paradise too;
wild and free,
the sentiments of fools.

Some days,
the past has no reprieve.
The world was ours,
and for that, we can grieve.

March 8

Good Call

The phone rings for two reasons:

good news
or
bad news.

It's a crapshoot lately.
A missed call and you're left

guessing
or
wondering.

Who died or who was born?
I answered on the first ring,

hoping
and
wishing

that it would be a good call.

March 9

Lost

Surely, you've lost someone before,
who hasn't?
Misplaced souls are a dime a dozen.

Saying they're lost, like they'll be found,
so innocent.
A parent, a friend, a boss, a cousin.

For that time of grieving you feel,
so special.
But, the truth is you're not alone.

Loss, changes to the word gone,
forever.
Then that grief, sinks like a stone.

March 10

New Style

Your hair is longer
and your smile wider.
Hard to believe
it's been twelve years.
I still think about you,
from time to time,
or when I hear that song
or see a Shelby '69.
Who thought back then
we'd ever go out of style?
But seeing you now,
you look better in that smile.

March 11

Um...

Numb,
struggling to feel,
captured by lies
that promised to heal.

Dumb,
unable to think,
what free will existed
gone in a blink.

Crumb,
all that is left
of a meager salary
of the fooled and bereft.

Scum,
now it is praised
by desolate hearts
whose voices are raised.

March 12

4,322

4,322 years ago,
something happened.
Just like 4,322 minutes ago,
something happened.
Every moment
is history in the making.
What kind of future
are you creating?

March 13

Fertilizer

How isolated we are,
thinking our problems
are the only to exist.
The grass may be greener,
but you don't know
how they fertilize that shit.

March 14

Night & Day

The moon and the sun,
both in the sky,
each on their side,
shining a light.
Working overtime
and early to rise,
celestial bodies
sharing the time
between night
and the promised day.
Complete opposites
with so much to say.
Perhaps they know,
how more light can aid,
lift up some souls,
and make darkness fade.

March 15

BS & S

Okay, so politics has
NEVER been civil,
but it would be nice
to think
mankind has gotten
a little
better
than having to stab
a leader
to death.

Maybe, mankind
tried to compensate,
thinking all problems
could be solved
with bullshit
and
smiles.

March 16

Cereal

You used to make fun of me
for stocking up.
It's not like I was a prepper,
I just couldn't pass
up a deal.
Every empty space,
a box of cereal,
cabinets full of pasta,
and twenty gallons of water,
minimum.
Okay, maybe my knife collection
screamed a bit of doomsday,
but really,
who's laughing now?

March 17

Three Tours

Three tours in war zones
and you think you've seen it all.
Destruction, reconstruction,
hope, loss, and regimes fall.

You're a hero and a villain,
there's no in between.
You've killed, you've saved,
and adapted to what you've seen.

Back home won't look the same
and back there will haunt your dreams.
While all the folks you fought for
are busy making memes.

Your voice has not been heard,
but you've learned there is a way
to make the masses listen,
just blow them away.

March 18

Fellow Traveler

I don't need the road less traveled,
I just need the road you're on;
I'd give up safer travels
to be the one you want.

To me, there is no choice
because with you by my side,
the journey could be hell
and I'd still decide to ride.

Whatever comes our way,
or what the Fates have in store,
every bump, curve, or closure,
would make me love you even more.

March 19

The cRaZE

Blink and you'll miss it,
that story below the fold,
the one scrolling quickly,
or that just won't load.

Shut off the tv,
turn down the volume,
chuck the computer
right out the window.

Good news is hard to find
these days
since bad news
became the craze.

March 20

Tickin'

I'll never wear it,
the watch you gave me,
but sometimes,
I come across it,
wind it,
hold it to my ear,
and listen to it tick.

It's not my style,
meaning it's far too nice.

With my propensity
to walk into things,
I know it would shatter.
There's no one to give it to,
and I wouldn't be able to part
with this material memento
that still holds a tick
of your heart.

March 21

Smoke

I used to love cigarette smoke
before my lungs aged,
before my heart broke,
when our love raged
and our souls spoke.

Smoke and love warm
from the inside out,
but both do harm,
burning a route
and raising alarm.

I used to love you
before all the tears,
before I knew
it was all smoke & mirrors
concealing what was true.

March 22

B.P.M

Sixty beats per minute,
that's the average rate
whenever I'm with you
in a contented state.

140 for you,
cool as can be,
curled in a ball,
happy with me.

No matter the rate,
our hearts beat in time,
backbeat and bass,
you are my reason and rhyme.

March 23

Oasis

That's a lot of blank terrain ahead.
Lined pages of desolate desert,
just waiting to be fed.

Ideas dry up in the sand,
the sun scorches already yellowed pages.
The pen searches desperately for land
while the poet emulates sages.

Who knew it wasn't a mirage after all?
The oasis was there,
waiting for me to fall.

March 24

Famous ★ Duos

Patience & Fortitude,
rhythm & blues,
wait & hope,
win & lose.

Heart & soul,
set & rise,
lock & key,
your green eyes.

Fish & chips,
false & true,
cats & spinsters,
me & you.

March 25

Option

Some tragedies
have no cure;
time won't heal,
words won't help,
love can't close
wounds so deep.
Walk on wounded
or succumb.
These are
the only options.

March 26

Long in the Tooth

Growing up is hard to do
when you never were a child
and never searched for you.
No days spent going wild,
no such thing as stolen youth,
no time spent coming-of-age.
Being born long in the tooth
should become all the rage.

March 27

Ghosted

Ghosted, you don't even know
the meaning of the word.
You think it's bad losing touch?
Try living disturbed.
Boo, who are you waiting for?
The line is dead.
Don't call, don't write, don't text,
just keep your demons fed.

March 28

Necesidades

Necesito amarte para siempre,
como necesito respirar,
como las olas necesitan rodar,
y las estrellas necesitan brillar.

Si me preguntas, ¿por qué?
la respuesta está en la forma
en que sopla el viento,
en que late mi corazón,
en que gire el mundo,
en cada sentimiento.

Necessities

I need to love you forever,
like I need to breathe,
like the waves need to roll,
and the stars need to shine.

If you ask me why,
the answer is in the way
the wind blows,
the way my heart beats,
the way the world turns,
in every feeling.

March 29

Insomnia

Death comes just like sleep
if one is lucky enough,
life's insomnia.

March 30

Shoveling

Snow is still falling
when my shovel scrapes pavement.
The sun behind the clouds,
barely risen, makes a statement.
Birds flitter by,
singing their morning song,
heading to the feast,
flapping through the throng.
I take a break from my work
and set the shovel down
to listen to the peace
in nature's surround sound.

March 31

Extinction

The Tasmanian tiger,
the golden toad,
the heath hen,
their demise forbode.

Quagga, dodo,
baiji, and vaquita,
no longer here,
soon to be joined by the cheetah.

Spix macaw and the great auk,
unjustly killed by man,
lucky to have made the ark,
but succumbed to God's plan.

The dinosaurs are done,
simply fossils in the ground,
a memory in a museum,
empty of fury and sound.

Was it that they couldn't adapt
or is mankind to blame?
I'm sure it's a bit of both
that makes all extinction the same.

Perhaps the white male,
needs to take heed,
before he's on the list
of a vanishing breed.

April 1

Labeled

I've been labeled:

> a dyke,
> a bitch,
> a daughter,
> a sister,
> a lover,
> a writer,
> a poet,
> a brother,
> a friend
> to name a few.

Scratch off the labels
and you're left with
unbranded, unadulterated,
pure,
human being.

April 2

Not Funny

Is there anything
funny anymore?
I hesitate to open my mouth
in fear of insulting the door.
I get the jokes
might be insensitive,
but when did laughter
become hypersensitive?
I told this joke,
just the other day,
thought it was the bomb,
would blow the audience away,
but like is often
the comedienne's case,
the joke was on me
and blew up in my face.

April 3

What a Ride

Freedom,
vibrations,
pavement,
scintillations,
night air,
dark sky,
headlight,
hair flies,
arms wrapped,
motor purrs,
leather jackets,
feelings stir.

April 4

Missing

Twenty years gone by
and still an empty space.
A collection incomplete
stares me in the face.
A single title missing,
but a giant, gaping hole.
A story never finished
will always haunt the soul.

April 5

Art

Fingers once nimble
move swiftly to create art;
wow, those hands have lived.

April 6

Scratch That

I remember the day you ~~left~~ died.
My heart ~~was so bereft~~
was so broken, I cried.
My soul was ~~wrecked~~
~~shattered~~
~~broken~~
gone.
~~I felt like I'd been decked.~~
~~My whole being, battered.~~
~~A love no longer spoken.~~
A sunless, empty dawn.

April 7

Those Eyes

My eyes have been glued to your lips
all
night
long.
I'm no better than those guys
coming on so strong.
They watch your every move,
but never above the neck.
While it's worth the view,
they're missing half the trek.
With hopes of drowning in the sheets,
they're pouring on the lies,
while they only place I want to drown
is hidden in those eyes.

April 8

Always Shoot the Messenger

I debated whether or not
I should tell you what I saw;
the eye of the beholder
is quite known for its flaw.
Your heart knows better
than my cool, collected mind,
so if I share my thoughts,
you'll think me less than kind.
But, here's the truth you should know,
even if you don't believe a single word,
that girl will rip your heart out
and trample it like a wild herd.

April 9

Fantasy

Fantastical lands
filled with magic and creatures
got nothing on Earth
and all Her beautiful features.
We've got heroes and villains
and magic our own
in moments of love
and in every rolling stone,
rolling river, lush tree,
epic battle, and secrets from the past.
Give me reality
since the fantasy won't last.

April 10

What a Drag

A little rouge,
some tape,
and a tuck.
The prettiest belle
with the balls
who won't give
a single fuck.

A little booze,
some cash,
and a knife.
Who knew that she would
be doing more
than just lip-synching
for her life?

April 11

Fred & Bob

Like a sister,
you know,
the younger annoying one.
You certainly
won a place
in my cold, distant heart.
You're family,
you know,
a kind soul, bar none.
Annoying or not,
the years
will never tear us apart.

April 12

Just Words

Apologies are just words
and words are just creations,
man-made aberrations,
signifying exactly,
more or less,
whatever lies
beneath the surface
of lies.

April 13

Mother Nature's Song

It's not that the mountains
are blanketed in snow
or that the sun beats down
on blooms that will grow.

The trees can stand still,
or with the wind they can blow,
and just as sure as the seasons,
the tides will ebb and flow.

The bluest of skies
and the greyest of clouds,
rocks stuck with moss,
acting as shrouds.

Her beauty is there
in every living thing,
so open your heart
and let Mother Nature sing.

April 14

Demons A-Z

We're all so concerned
with demons of our own
we sometimes forget
we're not all alone.
From Aamon to Ziminiar,
and every one in between,
there's a friend for every soul
that's a little less than pristine.

April 15

This Old House

Boxes packed,
floors swept,
voices echo,
in empty space.
Once a home,
now a house.
Memories, once
contained in
these four walls,
now live
within our hearts.

April 16

Stay with Me

Misery loves company
and that's why you stayed with me
just long enough to bring your doom
with gloom and catastrophe.
Jaded, wilted, morbidly obtuse,
unhappiness is contagious
and contentment of no use.

April 17

Poetry in Motion

My eyes move
as you move
and each motion
sends me to the moon.
Those eyes,
catch mine
and soon,
we are
poetry in motion.

April 18

bOOm

This place was built on dynamite.
Fuse lit, the founders walked away.
Figure it out on your own
and if you don't like it,
don't stay.
Sparks close in
on that red stick;
no heroes remain
darkness
looms.
boom

April 19

Last First Time

Could there ever be a day
when there will be no more firsts?
All has been said and done before,
every idea and notion nursed.
Will boredom haunt our minds
or will freedom free our hearts
to love without prejudice
like they should have from the start?

April 20

Fifth

It's your fifth time
scrolling through the feed,
and then back to the news.
A tear runs down your cheek
and you stumble to bed,
grasping a bottle of booze.
Numbing the world outside,
and finding peace within,
impossible to do
even with a fifth of gin.
Another day of rain,
the sun behind the clouds,
the news is still the same.
Every comment below
gets worse than the last,
always shifting blame.
Today, there is a fifth,
tomorrow, maybe more,
but the fact that this is normal
is what cuts you to the core.
It's your fifth time
stumbling out the door

to the world outside.
It's the fifth year in a row
there hasn't been a single day
you haven't cried.

April 21

In Your Eyes

People forget,
or choose to ignore,
the fact that the eyes
can't see all that's in store.

What one person sees,
another does not,
but which one is right?
What truth is sought?

The eye sees it right,
but the mind reads it wrong,
so rather than fight,
they should seek to get along.

April 22

Good Company

The last concert I went to
still vibrates in my bones.
The crowd I could do without,
but the melodies I keep on loan.

There isn't much I miss
from the time before the end,
but music doesn't feel the same,
without the company of a friend.

April 23

Too Many Syllables

I have never been a fan of sonnets;
there are too many syllables to fill,
then there's the talk of flowers and bonnets
and ramblings of love and hearts beating still.

I've got to be honest with you, my dear,
it's no flower to which I must compare
the beauty of seeing you drink a beer,
or laughing, so completely unaware

that your infectious illumination
is what makes not just my world go around,
but powers all this planet's rotation
and keeps this lost soul, firmly on the ground.

Those words captured what I set out to do,
which was basically to say, I love you.

April 24

Fall

It's easier to fall in love
than to fall out,
but given the choice,
I'd rather not
fall at all.

April 25

David Copperfield

Pearl Hawthorne (b. circa 1873)
read a book that belonged to B.J. Mull
back sometime in 1880.
The first time Pearl finished it,
was in October 1903.
She made a note in the back
for future readers to see.
In 1934, she read it again,
perhaps more carefully,
but made a note once more
of her literary feat.
Between pages 254 and 255,
tucked so casually,
are newspaper clippings
from about 1950.
Did Pearl put them there
around the age of 70
or did a new reader
leave them thoughtlessly?
The history is there
and the mystery is free.

What mark shall I make
now the book belongs to me?

April 26

Soul'd

Sold the sofa
so we could eat.
Sold the guitar
to make rent.
Sold the tv
for gas.
Sold the car
so she
wouldn't have to
sell her soul.

April 27

Carpe Diem

Golden leaves,
green eyes,
brown grass,
blue skies.
Black fur,
rosy cheeks,
yellow sun,
white peaks.
Pink blanket,
clear breeze,
the colors of a day
we were meant to seize.

April 28

What a Way to Go

It's so cold,
the heart skips a beat,
make that two,
then, a sudden heat.
The snowbank
is a warm place to rest.
A body fits perfectly
in a white frozen nest.
Above, in the dark,
snowflakes mix with stars.
It's like floating in space,
speeding in cars.
Eyelids grow heavy
and old wounds mend.
How unfortunate that soon,
this moment will end.

April 29

No Joke

A white man,
a Black man,
and an Indigenous man
walk into a bar.
Bellies up,
drinks orders,
stories shared,
a trip on par
with countless others
that leave the men
a little closer to broke,
but full of laughter,
and a mutual understanding
that brotherhood is no joke.

April 30

Mirror

My face shatters
into a million little pieces
as I pull back
my bloodied fist
and I think,
did I break the mirror,
or did it break me?

May 1

Doing Time

I did a stint
in nature's jail,
trees and leaves,
fur and tail.
Captured by awe
and held by vine,
lost observance,
my evil crime.
Reformed and recluse,
I'll live my days
in all Her beauty
and buds of May.

May 2

For All

Some 250 years ago,
women and slaves,
the poor and outcast,
joined a battle
seeking freedom.

Duped by those in power,
some 250 years later,
the underdogs still think
that "for all"
applies to them.

May 3

Just Beachy

Life is just beachy today,
salt air, sandy shores,
and a cool breeze.
The clouds could come,
but the grey can't stay
in a life of ease.
Rolling waves, crashing hearts,
summer daze, boardwalk carts,
give us more,
please.

May 4

15 Years

It sat there for fifteen years
collecting dust, rust,
and bad vibes.
Scrap, junk, a murderer
with rotted rubber
and broken spokes.

I've sat here for fifteen years
collecting loss, misery,
impossible to describe.
A scrappy junkie
with rotted veins
and no fire to stoke.

May 5

Kick-Ass Chica

Making a go at this thing known as life
almost never works out the way you plan.
Unfortunately, for chaos and
ruin, they won't know what hits them
as you grow to
become the most kick-ass chica
every girl wants
to be.
Hold on to that fire and you'll never
lose.

May 6

Styx & Stones

Sticks and stones
used to be all
that could break bones
until tweets and posts
turned some words
into prideful boasts
and guns and knives
fueled by hatred
ended up taking lives
and breaking more bones
than any words
or sticks and stones.

May 7

Good Man

She needed a good man,
one who could handle
all the ups and downs.
One not afraid to love,
to honor, to be a clown.
She needed a good heart
with only love to give
and intentions pure and true.
You may not take the trash out,
but she got lucky with you.

May 8

You're Doing It Wrong

That patriotism
you wear on your sleeve
isn't as true
as you'd like to believe.

That hatred
you have in your heart
was born from
whatever tore you apart.

That rage
has simmered so long.
That patriotism,
you're doing it wrong.

May 9

Always Blame Your Mother

Tying my shoe,
signing my name,
reading a book,
you're to blame.

Thinking for myself,
standing my ground,
loving animals,
appreciating nature's sounds.

How to bake,
even though I don't.
How to cook,
but probably I won't.

You put ideas in my head.
You put a hammer in my hand.
You put food on the table
and taught me to put a seed in the land.

You showed me what can be saved,
and to leave what cannot be
and that helping others
can never come, before helping me.

Because of you,
I know unconditional exists
and even when you're gone,
your memory will persist.

Fighting the world,
walking through flame,
every success,

you're to blame.

May 10

Sisyphus

If there is anyone
who knows how that guy felt,
it's me.
Each day, the task starts,
the same as the day before,
constantly uphill
with the heaviest boulder
ever
made.
I like trickery as much
as the next king,
but surely my punishment
is not the same.
My lot in life is set,
like his in death,
not for my actions,
but for my tax bracket.
So, if there is anyone
who knows how that guy felt,
it's me.

May 11

It's a Riot, Grrrl

You can only
be beaten down
so far
before you rise up,
fight back,
speak louder.

Crowds gather,
voices blend,
and that fire you set to the world
begins to mend.

Here in the trenches,
it's a riot, girl.

May 12

Drug Money

They'll only use the money for drugs.
Insulin, EpiPens, and the such.
Why don't they get another job
if they need their drugs so much?

How greedy and selfish they are
wanting my hard-earned dollars;
minimum wage is more than enough
to support their blue collars.

So, they've got mouths to feed,
well I've got some too,
and caviar isn't cheap
for a party of 102.

I don't believe in handouts,
but tax breaks sure are nice,
and stepping on the little guy
is such a bargain price.

May 13

Eidetic Memory

The back of my eyelids
are the perfect canvas
to replay every thought,
every memory, every image
that have been imprinted
not only in my mind,
but permanently,
in my heart.

May 14

Cons

The sun came up today,
blinding me through the window,
urging me from the bed
far before I was ready though.

The shower turned cold,
well lukewarm at least,
and my meager breakfast
was far from a feast.

Back to the mindless grind
that I left a few hours ago.
If I could quit this job,
life would be better, I know.

May 15

Pros

The sun came up today,
an absolutely marvelous feat
for a 4.603-billion-year-old star
that continues to produce heat.

The shower turned cold
before I was done,
but I'm luckier than others
who have no water to run.

Back to the mindless grind
that helps pay the bills,
but happiness isn't in money,
it's in how we climb these hills.

May 16

Small Talk, Smiles, and Lies

I've never been lonelier
than when I'm in a crowded room.
Glasses clinking, chatter, food
are all signs of impending doom.
The corner is too obvious
a place to run and hide,
so I throw myself into the horde,
and rot away inside.
Do they even know,
what exists behind the masks?
Since truth and lies bleed together
in the questions no one asks.

May 17

One Night Stand

One night,
after the movies,
I was waiting for the bus.
It was cold,
the bus was late,
and the only ones there were us.

It was late
and dark,
and this was the
last bus of the night.
Our breath steamed,
the bus appeared,
its headlights were so bright.

The door opened,
you signaled
that I should get on first.
One step,
two steps,
and then the bubble bursts.

The driver spoke,
directly at you,
"I'm not driving your kind."
I looked at him
and I looked at you,
then made up my mind.

One step,
two steps,
I got off the bus.
I felt warm,
the bus was gone,
and the only ones were us.

What a dick,
what a prick,
damn, that racist rift.
You looked at me,
I looked at you,
"wanna' share a Lyft?"

May 18

Loca Motive

Relentless and ruthless,
you won't stop
until you get
exactly what you want.

¿Sabes lo que quieres?
¿Que no harías?

Your brain is on fire,
your tongue is a liar,
you're stuck in this haze,
your brain is a maze.

No puedes escapar
las voces dentro de tu cabeza.

Less than pure,
your motive rattles.
crazy, loca, crazy
Ruthless and relentless.

May 19

Evergreen

I knew I liked you
from the start,
the way you treated her,
stole her heart.
It soon became clear,
there was more to be seen,
your heart and soul
are surely evergreen.
How lucky she is
to call you wife
and lucky am I
that means you're in my life.

May 20

Duel

Guns drawn,
like the Old West,
except this time,
there are bullet proof vests.
Fast draw,
a modern-day duel,
not for honor or pride,
but solely for the fool.

May 21

Wallet

I carry your picture
in my wallet.
An old-fashioned gesture
or whatever you want to call it.
It's faded and creased,
but your image remains.
It's not like I need it,
since you run in my veins.

May 22

Soul-Bending

Dark humor
and unhappy endings
make my heart
go on pretending
that life ain't so bad
and I can manage fending
off the blackness
that has my soul bending.

May 23

The Butterfly Effect

You could bat your eyes
in Tokyo,
and all the way back in the states,
I'd know
it's you who makes my heart
still grow
and the butterflies never stop
below.

May 24

Bullet Proof

This stain won't ever come out;
once it sets, there's no hope.

One second it wasn't there,
then the next it was,
like one second you were,
and now you're not.

That soul will never return;
once that light dies, there's no hope.

Thoughts and prayers,
vacant stares,
tears enough to fill
the drying seas
and
still
no
hope.

The hate will never end;
once it sets, there's no hope.

How could you look her in the eyes?
How were you prepared to die?
How did you find the strength to pull it?

The answer is clear:
hate is alive,
the proof is in the bullet.

May 25

Mehtcao

A few raindrops fall
as you kneel beside
the pup on your leash.
A smile breaks out,
covering your face,
and I think to myself,
this overcast day
has its first spot of sun.

May 26

Hope & Hell

Places and people
are a blur.

Moments and memories
unable to stir.

Feelings and fears
left unsure.

Hope and Hell
both willing to lure.

May 27

Some Friends

Some friends come and go
and some seem always to stay
deep within our hearts.

May 28

Man V. Nature

Man killed by man
and no one bats an eye.
Instead, he wipes a tear
while innovating fresh ways to die.

Man starves alone,
and everyone turns an eye.
One man's despair
is another man's high.

Man faces Her,
and it opens up his eyes
as Mother Nature levels
all mankind's lies.

May 29

Coming Up for Air

What a feeling,
when every page is filled
with ink, sweat,
and ideas that have spilled.
Blank pages can
cause bouts of despair,
but filling up a notebook
is like coming up for air.

May 30

Crooked Road

A crooked road waits
for a weary traveler
to misplace his step.

May 31

Leucanthemum Vulgare

Pressed between the pages
of *Bulfinch's Mythology,*
a daisy lost for ages
has become a myth itself.

Maybe it was Jupiter,
just playing a game,
or Cupid's mistake,
the recipient of blame.

Beowulf and Arthur,
both honorable men,
willing to die for
any noble cause.

Then there's the daisy
we plucked from the earth
that early spring morn,
full of cheer and mirth.

The greatest love tale
that's never been told
is on a small scale
contained in petals of white.

No drama or feud
when two souls become one,
so let the gods yawn
at our flower in the sun.

June 1

A Tree

A seed,
planted in the spring.
The promise of life
dangling on string.

>A change,
>out with the native,
>in with the new.

>>A cry,
>>from a babe or mother,
>>father, sister,
>>or brother.

A drop,
of rain, or maybe blood.
A sapling survives
drought and flood.

>>A town,
>>built on sweat, blood,
>>and fears.

A woman,
chosen to die
whether she tells a truth
or a lie.

A tree,
rooted, standing tall
before you or I
were standing at all.

A beast,
created by his father
and his father's father.

A man,
born in the wrong time
so that his skin's color
makes his life a crime.

A life,
taken by those
with no right to take.

A mob,
rooted in its belief,
not even a glimmer
of remorse or grief.

A tree,
standing witness in disbelief
as the noose falls
quicker than a leaf.

June 2

Goose

An oil-slicked tabby,
all legs,
but that was before I knew you.
My home was your home
long before I existed.
If fate had changed our courses,
my heart would still have a spot
for your purr, your fur,
your unrequited love.
My home was you,
long before I existed.

June 3

Rhiannon

I bought my first guitars
from a girl named Rhiannon.
I promptly learned the song
to add it to my canon.

Back then my fingers worked,
and each note rang through the night,
but now the notes fall flat
and my fingers put up a fight.

The guitar sits in a corner,
feeling the touch of dust more than hand,
and I wonder if it's as lonely
as this one-woman, washed-out band.

June 4

How it Ends

I've seen enough apocalypse flicks
to know how this ends.
The guy doesn't get the girl
and they don't ride off into the sunset.

I've read enough Stephen King
to know the horror.
Anyone can be a victim
and anyone can be a villain.

I've played enough games
to know what's real.
You win some
and you lose some.

I've seen enough sunsets
to know the beauty.
Just as sure as it sets,
to rise again is its duty.

I've survived enough storms
to know the pain.
That too shall pass
just like the rain.

I've lived enough life
to know its worth.
Simple acts of kindness
are the balance of Earth.

June 5

Another's Shoes

I always try to put myself
in other people's shoes;
no matter how ill the fit,
it's good to see other views.
But, no matter how hard I try,
there will still be some footwear,
so utterly rank and ratty,
that I'd rather keep my feet bare.

June 6

People & Things

That old vinyl
couldn't handle one more flip
and my favorite shirt,
I'd have worn it 'til it was just a strip.

My first baseball glove,
fell apart in my hand,
and my special pen,
dried up like the sand.

That *New Oxford American,*
has seen better days,
and don't get me started
on that ratty cap for the Braves™.

The things that we love
never stand a chance,
worn down and weakened,
by blows that do more than glance.

That's what makes people
better than things;
the harder you love them,
the more strength it brings.

June 7

Don't Remember

It's not easy
remembering things
other people don't.
In their eyes,
you're the one
who is crazy.
Maybe you are,
maybe you aren't,
but the good thing is
you can always hope
they'll forget you.

June 8

Polaris

There's a map inside my heart
that always shows the way,
and when I am lost on land or sea,
my compass points to you.
Shining brighter than all the rest,
you always light my way,
and no matter what I've seen or done,
I always find my way back to you.

June 9

Fishtail

A million times,
maybe that's an exaggeration,
but it's got to be close
to the actual calculation.
In rain, in snow,
in every kind of precipitation.
In sorrow, in anger,
and in all ranges of elation.
And once, just once,
your passenger was inebriation,
and before you knew it,
you lost your concentration.

June 10

Be a Man

Eventually you will
venture out on your own
and the boy you once were
needs to be a man, full-grown.
Just remember to be kind,
open-hearted, and true.
Seek answers, ask questions,
every day starts anew.
Plant seeds of
hope.
Love all you do.

June 11

Open Wounds

I always kept my wounds covered
and they took forever to heal.
With no air to breathe life
back into what hurts so much to feel.

I don't know how long it took
to realize I'd been marred
by years of poorly healed damage
that left me purely scarred.

June 12

The Key

I want you to know
there won't be a fight
when it's my time to go,
it'll be gently into the night.

Why try to evade
what is sure to be?
To live life unafraid
is surely the key.

June 13

Buckets of Tears

Trails,
and highways,
and buckets
of tears.

History
repeating,
playing
on fears.

Progress
changing,
working
the gears.

But you can't
take back
all the buckets
of tears.

June 14

Red Panda
Ailurus fulgens

Just chill, human,
you worry too much.
Don't forget to lounge
and sleep a whole bunch.
Take it from me,
the best way to sleep
is feet hanging down,
not making a peep.
I may have it easy,
being so cute,
but sometimes I struggle
eating my shoots.
This big bushy tail
can get in my way
and I've been known
to be frightened some days.
Some call me "lesser,"
but that's just a word;
the only thing that matters
is how beautifully I'm furred.

June 15

Workin' 9-5

Up before the birds,
but the coyotes aren't in bed.
Dimly lit blacktop
leads me where I head.

Sore muscles and rough hands
from work the day before
with no reprieve in sight
as I mop another floor.

I take a moment's rest
for water and a sigh,
and out the window view,
a runner passing by.

Dawn is finally breaking,
and I wonder how it feels
to make the choice to run
without the Devil on your heels.

June 16

Outcasts

I seem to be partial to the outcasts,
the free spirits, the lost souls.
Those are the ones who will outlast
all society's trolls.

Unique, diverse, or just frickin' weird,
beating to their own drums,
means they are sure to be feared.

No matter how odd they seem,
they live their lives freely,
and capture every dream.

Kindred spirits or perhaps just similar souls,
they refuse to live the lie.
While others try to fill in holes,
the outcasts question why.

June 17

Make Believe

I get it,
I mean, I used to run around too
with my arsenal,
decked out in gear,
waiting to get the enemy
in my sights.
The hero of my own story,
so valiant, so brave.

What a feeling!

But,
I was ten.
I grew up,
like you're supposed to.

So, while y'all
are still playing make believe,
those are real bullets.

June 18

Vignette

The sun felt good today,
it's easy to forget,
how warm the rays are
when you haven't got a fret.
The ease and the comfort
of a dusty vignette
and the constant promise
of what's not happened yet.

June 19

Patriotism

"It spelled narrowness—limitations."
-Jane Ellen Harrison

Children of the world unite
while proud boys and girls
look for ways to divide.
Standing for Queen & Country,
fighting for leader & despot,
patriots for the contrary.
A land for all (who fit the bill)
or a reason to be better
than those who won't swallow the pill.
My country 'tis of thee,
from sea to polluted sea
and made just for me.

June 20

33⅓

33 rotations per minute,
well, 33⅓ to be exact,
but who wants to deal
with fractions like that?
Roughly 600 times,
we'll go round & round
before we flip it over
and listen to new sound.
That's too much math though,
for my brain to do;
the only equation to solve
is me + you.

June 21

Hey, Satan

Hey, Satan, my man,
how's it hangin'
down south?
Things up here
are getting chilly;
I think snow
is coming soon,
or is that ash?

Hey, Satan, my friend,
could you spare
just a few flames?
I'm sure you've felt
some of these northern
winds blow
and seen those trees
swing and crash.

Hey, Satan, I'm sorry.
I didn't know
Hell froze over too.

June 22

Sequoyah

Do you think he ever imagined
a white fourth-grade girl
would take the time
to change her world,
study his syllabary,
let her wings unfurl?

An illiterate man,
limping along,
preserving his culture,
keeping strong
a nation so divided
by white man's wrongs.

Taking it into his own hands,
with the help of his young girl,
they brought literacy
and changed the world
by inventing a syllabary
that is a treasured pearl.

June 23

Flesh & Bone

Ownership is a mark
I do not wish to make
before leaving this plane.
Can't take it with you,
no one to leave it to,
so it ends up a dark stain.
What right would I have
to call something my own?
My soul is just passing through,
mere flesh and bone.

June 24

The Proof Is in the Tooth

Your toothmark
on my Emily Dickinson collection
is proof
that you could do anything
and I would still love you,
all because
your pawprint
on my beating heart
is proof
that I would do anything
for this ball of fur with sharp teeth.

June 25

Unrequited

How many boxes of tissues
have I gone through over Her?
Does She not know,
how she makes my emotions stir?
I would do anything
to save Her from ruin,
and still, She tries to kill me
from March through June.

June 26

Our Story

Clacking away
on your electric typewriter,
crafting a story
about a girl with a fake eye.
She was late,
for a very important date,
and you were gracious
to a young writer
honing her craft.

That story was shit,
and we both knew it,
okay, maybe some editing
could have helped.

But, how I would have loved
to autograph my first book
to one of my first readers,
one of my first fans,
the only man,
who ever mattered in my life.

Our story,
was not shit.

June 27

The Divide

We got
300 miles
and a carload
full of cardboard.

We got
pink knit hats
and little voices
to be heard.

We got
holes in our hearts
and fire in our souls.

We lost
friends & kin
fire's rising from the coals.

> We got
> 300 rounds
> and a truck bed
> full of napalm.
>
> We got
> red ball caps
> and declarations
> to be made.
>
> We got
> fear in our hearts
> and fire in the barrel.
>
> We lost
> friends & kin
> this country is in peril.

Can't you see we're right?
Can't you see they're wrong?
Been fighting for our rights,
been fighting for so long.
Can't you hear us yelling?
Can't you hear us scream?
The world as we see it,

can't be just a dream.

June 28

More than Just a Dream

Can't you see what's right?
Can't you see what's wrong?
We all deserve our rights,
shouldn't have to take this long.
Maybe we should listen
more than we should scream,
then one day this place could be

more than just a dream.

June 29

By You

Being loved by you
is exhilarating,
overwhelming,
full of hope.

Being left by you,
is heart-wrenching,
incapacitating,
empty.

June 30

What is Pride?

What is pride?
Is it the opposite of shame?
Is it living with yourself
and not distributing blame?

Do you wake up in the morning
and love the one you see
staring back from the mirror,
yearning to be free?

Is it the smile on your face
or the gesture small or grand?
Is it the love for self
and the love for fellow man?

One thing I can see
is that it's not parades & flags;
it's also not some dumb men
complaining about those "fags."

It's what is in your soul
and the product you create.
It's in the love you give,
but it's never in the hate.

July 1

Weighted

She just knew,
some women do,
but she took the test
and waited.

She had to do
what she didn't want to
and the way she felt,
she hated.

She thought some more,
tallying the score
and she knew that it
was fated.

It hurt her to the core
when they called her a whore,
but it was her choice,
so weighted.

July 2

To the Girl Who Sat in the Dryer
March 10, 2014

We spotted you through the window that night,
a gentle spin we took to look twice.
Questions tumbled through our minds,
is she drying her pants? They look nice.

You sat with your phone and pondered the screen.
Perhaps she needs to vent, or she didn't see the seat.
This could be a delicate situation, we think,
at least it's the bottom; sitting on top would be a feat.

If we asked her the problem, would she come clean?
Could we provide any help she might require?
Or, maybe she just found the warmest seat in the place.
Here's to proving normal is just a setting on the dryer!

-K2Au

July 3

Mr. Alighieri

Does he really think
his journey took him
any farther than earth?
He saw but nine circles
of a burning Hell;
that was just man's hearth.

What other circles exist
and what other sinners
were missing from his tour
that Virgil started too late?

Orpheus could not help
but divert his
temptation-driven eyes
and Dante could not help
but to believe
hopelessly grievous lies.

July 4

First

You're the first person I call
well, besides my mom,
whenever I have news
or something is just wrong.
You're the first hole in my heart
and the first patchwork too,
probably the first tears
that made me feel like a fool.

I fought for you at first,
then fought with you last,
but it didn't take long
to put it all in the past.
I loved you first,
but I hope he loves you forever
as long as he understands,
we have ties that don't sever.

July 5

Sunrise, Sunset

History is what shapes the future,
and still we relive the past,
unable to move forward,
unable to make hope last.

The future has never looked
so bleak and unprepared,
and the past has not reconciled
with what the present is paired.

Ready or not, tomorrow awaits.
Will the sun rise over hope
or will it set on despair?

July 6

Emily

Do you believe in love
at first read?
I think it was her dashes
that took the lead.

At first—her words
hit home.
Then—they made my lost
soul roam.

I'm sure we were
meant to be—
If only we had both lived
in the same century.

July 7

The Ocean

The ocean was quiet today,
only a few scraps of trash
washing up on shore.
Does that mean there is less
rolling in Her waves,
or simply that she learned
to stomach the polluted haze?
The ocean floated away
on heaps of human trash
that washed up every shore.

July 8

Sated

Dinner unfinished,
left to cool
with the wine.
Sheets tangled
warmed instead
by a heat divine.
A meal planned,
beautifully,
carefully plated.
One hunger left
while another,
completely sated.

July 9

NUM8ERS

The numbers don't look good,
but I never had a knack for that.
Ignoring simple truths
is what I've got down pat.
What's in a number?
After all, it's just a name
for a symbol of worthlessness
in a poorly marketed game.

July 10

Luster

I've taken a shine to you
and that's rare for me,
but I see a truth in you
that reflects back into me.

Life was lackluster before you
and now, I'm free to be me
because the lively luster of you,
is the cause of the glow in me.

July 11

Survive

Mortified, at first
to find out
the dark truth:
Chipmunks
eat
frogs
and
baby
birds.

I am sure it doesn't
happen often,
but this cute little creature
is not so harmless.

We all do
whatever it takes
to survive.

July 12

The Pocket Guide to Life

Wake up,
open your eyes,
live without fear,
reach for the skies.

July 13

Stories

We are in charge of our own stories
and yet, more often than not,
we allow others to tell our tales.
Our voices are drown out
by merciless streams of media
and pride leaking from epic fails.
Before long, a shell of what once was
is some remnant, unexplained, a story
once vibrant, but now absolutely pale
and just like the oldest stories in time,
the masses will have you lynched,
burned, or left hanging by a nail.

July 14

Balance

Can light exist
without the dark
or would human life
be stuck in park?

It'd be nice to rid
the world of pain,
but how would we know
what we'd have to gain?

Get rid of rape, murder,
and the need to rob,
since without some pain,
I'd be out of a job.

July 15

Too Hard

It's really hard,
pretending to care
and even harder
avoiding the vacant stare.
Sometimes the smile
is just too much,
so nodding the head
is the only crutch.
After a while,
I start to feel that itch
and it's time to give up;
I'm just a bitch.

July 16

Gauche

I like
that the societal norms
have you flustered.
It's a relief
that awkward is still
alive and floundering.
It's better
to know you don't fit in,
rather than forcing
a square peg
into a round hole.

July 17

For Which They Stand

They said,
"If you stand
for nothing,
you'll fall
for anything."

How wrong
they were.

Pretty sure
those "patriots"
fell for everything
and they'll stand
for it all.

July 18

Gap

Kindness oozes
from your pores,
a secretion
we all adore.
The gap between
your loving arms
is like a home,
safe and warm.
The way you care,
so pure and true
is a superpower
made for you.

July 19

What's Your Beef with Gloria Steinem?

I guess it's hard for me
to understand
what the big deal is
with not needing a man.
But, it's more than that,
it's a sense of pride
in being free to be
and not to hide.
Sure, I was raised in a
different time,
and in yours, my life
would be a crime.
But, is your way of life
able to compensate
for women who are beaten, owned,
and brutally raped?

July 20

Dame

I must have lived through the 20s
in another life of mine
since jazz music, fast women,
and fancy suits sound divine.
I know I'm a woman now,
but maybe I was a man back then,
so I hope I was more open-minded
than most of the other men.
Even if I had been a woman,
I'd have worn a suit just the same
and showed them all happily,
the power of a dame.

July 21

Forgotten Moments

There are so many moments,
people,
we think we'll never forget.
But we do.
In one space and time,
nothing
seems more important.
But that's not true.
Look at all the moments,
forgotten,
lost to time and space,
and void of you.

July 22

Fight Night

A consensual beatdown,
full of blood and sweat,
cheers, jeers, and spit,
and our eyes met.

The battle in the ring
ain't nothin' compared to
the one outside the ring,
between me and you.

Two hearts, KO'd long ago,
put down by constant toils,
but this battle is different.
To the victor, go the spoils.

July 23

Stagnant

The space
between covers
had grown stagnant.
Breath sucked right out
of a formerly
voracious movement.
A change of venue,
a change of heart,
but CPR
was never
administered.
So, breathlessly,
morbidly,
moldy ideas
crumble away
from the page.

July 24

Sudoku

Numbers one through nine
twenty-seven times align
and now, it's bedtime.

July 25

Look

Look into the mirror,
and the advice of a stranger
will pose a threat
to your sanity.
Look into your heart,
and the presence of darkness
will mount a war
against your vanity.
Look unto the world,
and the atrocities of man
will break your will
and impede tenacity.
Look to the darkened sky,
and the fire and brimstone
will be all evil needs
to hold veracity.

July 26

Heart Beat

I would never ask you
to give up something you love
for me.
Just like, I hope you
would never ask me to give up
something for you.
But, I know in a heartbeat,
I'd give up everything
I love
if it meant that your heart beat
a little lighter,
my love.

July 27

Just Another

Just another dead Indian,
another Black thug,
another dirty whore,
another political shrug.

Just another jobless hobo,
another job-stealing spic,
another Arab terrorist,
another bone to pick.

Just another distraction,
another scapegoat,
another cover-up,
another slit throat.

Just another day,
another grab for power,
another misleading leader,
another wilted flower.

July 28

In the Middle

Sold my amp,
but I still got a voice,
you'll hear us in the back;
you don't have a choice.
I can only hope
you hear what we say,
actually listen
to this area of gray.
Far to the sides,
you're bound to tip,
but here in the middle,
we have a better grip.

July 29

Bullets

My Remington
is poised,
ready,
aimed,
loaded.
I'm imagining
all the carnage,
wreckage,
damage,
destruction.
A few carefully placed bullets
and rapid-fire clicks,
pop a few caps,
and see which idea sticks.

July 30

Alone in the Dark

Being alone in the dark
illuminates the rest of life.
The silence feeds the soul
and lessens the strife.
Eyes wide open often miss
the secrets within the shadow,
but eyes pointed inward,
can help a garden grow.
We're all alone in the dark,
just feeling the way,
but we all contain a spark
that can turn night into day.

July 31

I Heard an iPhone® Buzz—When I Died—

I heard an iPhone® buzz – when I died –

The Stillness in the Room
Was like the Stillness in the Cloud –
Between the Heaves of Upload –
–
The Eyes around – had always been dry –
And Breaths were gathering firm
For that last Onset – when a snapchat
Be witnessed – in the Room –
–
I willed my passwords – Signed out
What portion of me be
Digital – and then it was
There interposed an iPhone –
–
With Blue – uncertain – stumbling Buzz –
Between the light – and me –
And then the iOS™ failed – and then
I could not see to see –

August 1

Sigue Tus Sueños

The best advice
I ever got
is on a quarter
of a torn envelope
in your handwriting,
written in Spanish,
but I see it
every time
I close my eyes.

August 2

Bald

It was your hair,
or the lack thereof,
that hit me.

You looked like shit

as you strolled up
so casually.
I knew about the booze,
but the drugs

hit you hard.

Now, you're bald,
hopelessly high,
and permanently scarred.

August 3

2nd **Rate**

I may be a second-rate bookseller,
perhaps a second-rate writer,
on the road to nowhere
who Google™ thinks is Autumn Spiders.

But, I'm a first-rate cat mom,
and a first-rate friend,
with first-rate morals
that I'm not willing to bend.

That road to nowhere,
may be my fate,
but the road you're on,
that doesn't even rate.

August 4

Bully

Change is essential,
that's not in question,
but if revolution is required,
mankind must learn a lesson:

History is a cycle,
always in motion,
the oppressed rise,
cause a commotion,
and once they reach
where they want to be,
it's time for the bullied
to become the bully.

August 5

Cats v. Dogs

I suppose I don't
write enough poems
about dogs.
But, it can't be helped
that cats are the ones
who hog
my heartstrings,
the words on the page,
so many thoughts.
Don't get me wrong,
dogs are cute too,
but they haven't got
that certain feline quality
that warms my heart
a whole lot.

August 6

Call it a Night

Life is full of choices,
as is death,
and the choice is mine to make
for when to draw my last breath.
You cannot dictate
whether or not I will fight
because when the dark comes,
it's time to call it a night.

August 7

Gamer

It's a thing now,
people pay money
to watch others
play videogames.

Back in the day,
I could watch you play
for hours on end
as you staked your claims.

You never charged a fee,
and it was I who felt rich
getting to spend time with you,
my hero, my big brother.

I don't know if it meant
anything at all to you,
but if there are any fees I owe,
I'd gladly pay my due.

August 8

Cu @ Oak Flat

It's all about the resources,
the money,
the greed.
How many assholes does it take
to mine copper?

One to steal the land,
one to tell the lies,
one to make promises,
one to take lives.

It's all about the importance,
a sacred
soul to feed.
How many voices does it take
to be heard?

One to yell,
one to explain,
one to show,
all to the break the chain.

August 9

We Can Make It

We've made it this far together,
and you're still here.
I think we can make it
through the whole year.
There's sure to be
more ups & downs,
but I'll try to deliver
more smiles than frowns.
Just remember though,
it's not all up to me
to keep you content
or change your mentality.

August 10

Hitlist

We all secretly
(or maybe not so much)
have a person
(or maybe more)
who we'd like to bring down
(maybe even kill).
It will never happen
(most likely)
since we show restraint
(more or less)
and a sense of decorum
(somewhat).
But still, it makes you think
(grimly)
that if we've all got one
(or more)
whose hitlist are you on?

August 11

EDNA

One time,
I was Edna,
an albino porcupine
who had a good life.
She needed a new branch,
so I offered up some help
and I was shocked to learn
I weigh more
than a porcupine.

"Okay, I'm Edna," I exclaimed,
and then a crack ensued
and we laughed so hard,
but Edna O.G.
didn't find it funny.

Who knew
porcupines
don't have
a sense of humor?

August 12

J

I think it's your laugh
that most people remember
or the smile that filled your face
and could warm the coolest December.
That's what we hold onto
because the grim reality
of what happened to you
seems an impossibility.
I think it's your laugh
that must get us through
as we carry it in our hearts,
knowing there's nothing we could do.

August 13

Behind the Curtains

Sometimes, I forget
there is a light
behind closed curtains.

So lost in my head,
deep in my fight,
darkness is certain.

You're not always
a ray of light,
but you bring me hope.

When all is wrong,
you make it right
just by opening the curtains.

August 14

Numbers Man

Not only did he know
how many minutes are in a year,
but he knew when to lease or own,
and all the numbers to fear.
He wrote hundreds of songs
which ended up being cut to forty-two
and all the numbers he crunched,
didn't change the fact that
when his number came up,
his final rent was due.

August 15

buveur d'encre

A thirst for words,
a hunger for knowledge,
an education better
than any old college.
Once you've tasted
that savory ink,
nothing else will quench
like that lexical drink.
Take a sip,
or gulp it down,
dive right in
to the best bar in town.

August 16

Obsolete

I remember the days
when you didn't need
a degree in quantum physics
just to fix something.
Any half-way intelligent,
hard-working Joe or Jill
could take a look
and figure out the repair.
The good old days are gone,
or maybe I'm not as smart
as I thought I was,
or perhaps, I too
am obsolete.

August 17

Next Track

That album you've listened to
one too many times on repeat
is imprinted on your brain
like a perfect vinyl, complete.
Then the single comes on the radio
and you're singing along,
nailing every word,
jamming like nothing's wrong.
The song comes to an end,
but on to the next track you go,
while the radio DJ
plays an ad for a show.

August 18

Market Basket Parking Lot

A late-night rendezvous
in a Market Basket parking lot
as headlights from the circle
shine light on two souls fraught
by what they thought
might be love,
but turned out
not.

August 19

Brotherhood

Brotherhood happens
when selflessness reigns
and good deeds prosper
over personal gains.

August 20

The Thrill

To some, the thrill
of hitting rock bottom
is so great
they've got to do it
again.

Falling from grace,
off the wagon,
down to Hell
is better than where
they've been.

At least the bottom
is solid ground
to stand firm,
prepare for battle
ahead.

When the thrill
is gone,
extinguished,
you might as well
be dead.

August 21

Spleen

I love you from tip to tip
and every inch in between.
I love every bone and muscle,
hell, I even love your spleen.
I love you through every chaotic moment,
and every breath made serene.
But, the words, "I love you,"
could never express what I mean.

August 22

Light Years

I never missed you more
than when you were right next to me
and yet,
light years away
from who we used to be.

August 23

Sublime

Forget the sun rising and setting
or a fresh blanket of snow,
a gentle rain in spring
to make the flowers grow.
Those leaves of golds and reds,
and the waves crashing in
on a white sandy shore
to wash away the sin.

All Her beauty surrounds us
at any given time,
but those who forget to listen
miss out on the sublime.

August 24

Discrimination

My skin may be white,
but the color of my faded,
　　　　dirty clothes
　　calls for disdain
　　just the same
as the color of his dark,
　　　　beautiful skin
　　and her fated
　　　　anatomy
　　and their old,
　　　　saggy skin.

　　Discrimination
　　　does not
　　　　discriminate.

August 25

Voluptuous

I want to get to know
every rounded curve,
every nook and cranny,
every single nerve,
and examine them
with awe and verve
until that voluptuous brain
gets the credit it deserves.

August 26

High Horse

How's the view up there?
That horse looks mighty tired
of carrying your worthless ass around.
If I were you,
I think I'd do my best
to keep those who carry me,
firmly on the ground.

August 27

listen

There has never been a better time
for people to open their eyes and listen;
a little work with one's hands,
could make the grime, glisten.

August 28

Shell

Today,
the world stopped turning,
and I,
could not be stopped.
The sun
darkened in the sky,
the end
growing ever near,
and while
my soul died long ago,
my body
drudged on forever.

August 29

The Secret Lives of Books

Stacks and tomes clutter the room
and blow gently in the cool breeze,
as if reading themselves.
Some may see the room
and think there is not a soul about,
but the secret lives of books
ensure this ghostly atmosphere
is the most lively place around.

August 30

Scrap

All the little pieces
that used to be whole
are parts scattered
in a junkyard so full.
One man's treasure
is another man's trash
to burn in the barrel
and float among the ash.

August 31

Fat & Old

You used to be so skinny
before you were filled
with knowledge and age.
Words and ink
fattened you right up
with every turn of the page.
It's not that I didn't
like you looking so slim,
but it seemed hard to gauge.
Now, it's clear to me
these yellowed lines are filled
with the wisdom of a sage.

September 1

Firework

Your celebration,
your bombs bursting in air
are another's devastation,
still you light up without a care.
What a pretty sight,
all those colors in the sky,
who cares if a fright
causes another to cry?
Bang, bang, like a gun.
Boom, boom, like a drum.
Shake, shake, it's no fun.
To the past, succumb.

September 2

By Any Other Name

Does the fiddle ever get mad
at being called a violin,
or is the violin ever shamed
by a fiddle mistaken for a twin?

A few small differences
and some can't tell them apart,
but what difference does it make
if they're both played from the heart?

September 3

Snapshots

Little snapshots,
blurred images,
faded, but ever-present scars,
dirt flying, blood flowing,
ears ringing,
and you,
dying
in my

arms.

September 4

Title

Call me "Crazy,"
but I got my first taste
of "Strawberry Wine"
off a tape deck
on the "Chattahoochee"
under a "Moonlight Sonata."
And, I "Never Will" forget
looking into "Them There Eyes"
on "A Night in Tunisia"
as a "Songbird"
flew through the "Spiderwebs"
and, like a "Drop in the Ocean,"
"She Used to Be Mine."

"In a Week,"
"One Week,"
I got "Caught Up in You,"
"Behind Blue Eyes,"
that "Gypsy,"

that "Smooth," "Gold Dust Woman,"
took me to the "Otherside."

Now, "I Can't Get Started"
in "A Little Dive Bar in Dahlonega,"
but "I Know Where I've Been"
and even "Walking in Memphis,"
there's a "Light in the Hallway"
that will always "Take Me Home"
to my "Beautiful Trauma."

September 5

Chicken Scratch

By the time this poem is typed,
the thought, the feeling
will be gone,
and the scribbles on the page,
undecipherable,
will long
for that feeling, that thought,
once visceral
and strong,
but now empty and lifeless
with nowhere
to belong.

September 6

Down Payment

I'd like,
if I could,
to apologize now
for the bad days
in the future
when I'll wear a scowl.
Think of it
as a down payment
on future happiness
and the promise
that you'll forever
fill me with bliss.

September 7

Two Days Ago

The message came through two days ago,
but I wasn't there to receive it.
Would it have made any difference
if open ears were there to believe it?

Urgency beckoned through a shaky voice
as the sun set from coast to coast,
but by the time the sun downed twice,
you never got the help you need the most.

September 8

Skip the Sage

This house is haunted
by your laughter
echoing on
in your afterlife.
I'll skip the sage
and embrace the dark
to keep your spirit
within my heart.

September 9

Callused

Back in the day
callused hands
meant a hard day's work.
A tired body,
a happy soul.

Today the calluses
rot away the flesh
and worked to the bone,
the body is tired
and the soul a wretch.

September 10

Waldeinsamkeit

Sunlight breaks through the canopy
and acorns lay down a beat,
crashing to the leaves
that crunch under my feet.

Babbling brooks,
chittering creatures,
creepy crawlies,
some of Her best features.

No traffic, no noise,
just my breath and soul
and a peaceful vibe
to make me whole.

September 11

Wonderland

The rabbit hole
of pharmaceuticals
leads to Wonderland.
That smile,
only stays so long
as the drugs wear off
and the side-effects
linger on.

September 12

True Purpose

Together, we carry the weight
of the world on our backs
and when one person suffers,
it's the right thing to do
to pick up the extra slack.

These hateful words can cut
deeper than a knife,
but hatred leads to nowhere.
We all know that it's love
that's the true purpose of this life.

September 13

Feral

Several times before,
she'd hiked these trails
and reached the end
with no perils
until that day,
filled with snow and gales,
early in May,
without proper apparel.
And that last hike,
was truly a fail
for she who forgot
Mother Nature is feral.

September 14

Deep Sleep

Sometimes,
I try not to wake you
when you need the sleep.

Other times,
I try to wake you
when you aren't making a peep.

Most times,
I like to watch you
like I'm a total creep.

All the time,
I dream I'm with you
and we're floating in the deep.

September 15

Armed Robbery

The first time
you held me in your arms,
it felt right,
my heart held no alarm.

The last time,
you pushed me away,
my heart knew
it was armed robbery.

September 16

The Answer

No person
is a simple answer.
The complexities
of heart & mind,
are the perplexities
that leave us blind
to what's behind
the simplicities
of one complex question:

Who are you?

September 17

Mentally Gone

I cry all the time now,
blame the puffy eyes on allergies,
the stuffy nose on nature,
but it's harder to find the cause
for this broken heart
without revealing the truth.

Physically here,
mentally gone,
a shell of a human,
I miss all day long.

September 18

Moonlight

Coyotes singing
one last chorus of the night.
Good morning, moonlight.

September 19

Sting

There was a bee
sitting on the bike seat
as a muggy Midwest summer
poured on the heat
and a little girl
ran back down the street,
avoiding the sting
she knew she would meet.

However, life is not fair,
and fate can't be beat;
a bee can still sting
even if you retreat.

September 20

Skeptical

The skeptic,
that's me,
and when I met you,
I couldn't believe
this man who stood before me.
Your intentions were pure,
your heart was golden,
and your resolve so sure.
Kindness,
compassion,
selflessness,
these words all pale
when stacked up
against you.

September 21

Debilitating

To some,
it means:
I can't function
before I've had my coffee.

To others,
it means:
how the hell,
do I find a way,
to get out of bed,
put a smile,
upon my face,
and convince myself,
it doesn't hurt?

May you never experience
the former
or be forced to survive
the latter.

September 22

Move to Bliss

Moving on
is like
inching into traffic,
dipping your toes in,
tentatively, teetering,
into the abyss
until you realize,
at full speed,
splashing,
all the way down,
you find bliss.

September 23

Past Its Prime

The dust settled
over a century ago
in a vacant house
on a lone country road.
A shattered window
and furniture askew,
a bone here and there,
and a tooth or two.

Preserved in time
with no one to hear
the story unfolded,
though why is unclear.
Two love birds
jaded by time,
severed the ties
of a love past its prime.

September 24

Growing up Golden

These four ladies
meant the world to me;
the only show worth watching
on that little tv.
Laughter and lessons,
cheesecake and sex,
learning to love
even your ex.
From St. Olaf to Sicily,
a Brooklyn gal or Georgia Peach,
life with these women
was always a beach.

September 25

Crack

Some days I'm falling apart,
cracking at the seams,
literally, figuratively,
and every meaning in between.

Mostly, I hold it together,
but a little slips away
since I can't even stop
the arterial spray.

September 26

A Trip around the Sun

Quite a year, Baby Girl.
Understand this, you don't have
infinite trips around the sun,
nor chances to soar amongst the stars. But,
never let that
stop you from defying the odds.

September 27

007

Bond gets such a bad rap,
that womanizing alcoholic.
Sure, his methodology
should never have been okay,
but at least he saved the world
unlike the rapists of today.

September 28

Brave Defeat

Bravery can be in the fight
or the moment of defeat.
Knowing the odds
is not the same as being beat.

It takes a stronger soul
to admit when it's the end
and only the cowardly
continue to pretend.

September 29

Again

Midnight,
again,
after I swore
I'd be in bed by ten.

Just like
when
I swore never
to be in your bed again.

September 30

Previously

Previously on life:

some embryos made it
and some did not.
The ones who did
gave this life a shot.
Some decided evil
was the way to go
and others thought good
made a better show.
Drama ensued,
plots moved along,
and those who survived
proved they were strong.

Tune in next week
to see how it ends,
or just enjoy life
with family and friends.

October 1

Confidence Artist

> The beauty,
> in the plan,
> the thought,
> the execution,
> the con man
> and all
> is in motion.
>
> A piece of art
> in all its glory
> to leave its mark
> broken and gory.

October 2

But You Want To

You didn't call
after that night
on the coast,
salty air,
watching the stars
from the bed of the truck,
waiting for the sun
while simultaneously
hoping the night
would never end.

I know why
you didn't,
you couldn't,
but you want to,
and that
will have to do.

October 3

Brick Wall

Try all you want,
you won't break it down,
these stones, set in place,
my heart they surround.
No need to wonder
what makes me tick,
you'll never get over
this wall made of brick.

October 4

Love Letters

Up in the attic,
under decades of dust,
letters are scattered
full of wanting and lust.
An affair to remember,
although it's forgotten
by the world at large
and time gone rotten.
For a moment in history,
two hearts beat as one
and a feeling like that
means that love isn't done.

October 5

Living in the Dark

The light goes out,
so abruptly,
and it's not that
I'm in the dark
that makes me
want to call it quits,
it's that I can no longer
see the page,
read the words,
make out the story,
and that
is far more tragic
that the simplicity
of living
in the dark.

October 6

Variety Show

Anthologies,
samplers,
generalists.
A little bit
of a lot of variety
can go a long way.

I worry about
those folks
who devote their lives
to one specialty.
The world
has so much
to offer,
to teach,
to enlighten.

Specialize
in
experiences,
and you'll be
an expert
of humility.

October 7

404 ERROR

A broken link,
poor communication
we tried to save,
but we're past salvation.
Talking in circles
or not at all;
we'll never fix
this firewall.
What we seek
cannot be found.
Request denied,
the network's down.

October 8

Not about Me

So you think you know me?
Read a few lines,
made some deductions,
saw the signs.
You are forgetting
what poetry must do,
it's not about me,
but a reflection of you.

October 9

Just One More

Ain't it crazy
how all the things we love
are tryin' to kill us?

We don't need 'em,
but we sure as hell
want 'em
knowing far too well
the consequences
of just one more.

October 10

Focus

I really dislike
not being able
to complete a single task
since my mind
can focus on nothing
but you.

October 11

I'll Think about It

I couldn't stop,
I know that,
but it doesn't change
the way it feels
to take a life.

You thought about it,
your last thoughts,
do I cross
or do I stay?

I'll think about it
'til my dying day.

October 12

Every Morning

A calling, a purpose,
a meaning,
hell, just a reason
to rise and move
every morning.

May you be a reason
for someone to rise
every morning.

October 13

But You Weren't There

Woke up this morning,
rolled over in bed,
but you weren't there.
Smelled coffee brewing,
went to the kitchen,
but you weren't there.
You left a note,
you ran to the store,
you'd be right back.
I turned on the news,
a tragic story unfolded,
right down the street,
a gunman entered the store.
Then, on the screen,
your car in the lot,
but you weren't there.
Casualties and bullets,
senseless bloodshed,
but you weren't there.

You couldn't be there.

After the gun smoke settled,
the gunman subdued,
the images emerged,
patrons and employees,
able to leave,
but you weren't there.
They set up a place
so loved ones
could reunite.

Got in the car,
drove downtown,
waited to see your face,
but you weren't there.
The crowd dispersed,
a few of us remained,
but you weren't there.
The officers approached,
hearts dropped,
but you weren't there.
Drove back home,
walked in the door,
but you weren't there.

You would never be there.

October 14

Holiday

Tied to the visor
on the driver's side of my car
is a rainbow ribbon
that's traveled near and far.
A peace sign design
that exudes who you are
and a memory in time
as rich as caviar.
You tied it to my wrist,
an accessory of pride,
but you need no occasion
to show your altruistic side.
From the first time I met you,
your generosity was a guide,
a holiday from the hateful
and the safest place to hide.

October 15

TTFN

Left behind,
out of sight,
out of mind.

Closed doors,
open wounds,
unfinished wars.

Sleepless nights,
empty days,
hopeless fights.

Separate ways,
broken hearts,
bitterness stays.

October 16

Concert in the Park

bucket drums,
subway thrums,
summer stench,
park bench,
wailing soul,
light pole,
green grass,
shiny brass,
night sky,
music flies

October 17

Wonderin' & Questionin' & Prayin'

Wondering
eats the soul
like
questioning
rots the heart
like
praying
digs a hole
that
you created
from the start.

October 18

Starstruck

Speechless,
my heart races,
excitement bubbles.
I've been waiting
all day
to see that face.

I should be embarrassed
to be this starstruck,
but I can't help
how you make me feel.

How lucky I am,
my Hollywood dream,
coming home to you,
is real.

October 19

Frozen Heart

When you've been out of the cold so long,
you forget just how bitter
the wind can be.

Safe and warm,
memories of a different time,
but they can't bolster enough heat
to keep the frigid temps
at bay.

Would it have been better
never to have left
the arctic in the first place?

A frozen heart
should never thaw.

October 20

Yesterday, Today, and Tomorrow

Today starts anew,
wishing yesterday away.
Tomorrow, can't stay.

October 21

Headache

Throbbing,
that's my head today,
although I remember,
vaguely,
it was a different body part
last night.

Another night
of regrets
and empty bottles,
headaches on top of headaches
masking pain;
it's not right.

It'll be all right,
tomorrow or the next time
I feel that ache
maybe that bottle
will be too far away,
out of sight.

what a plight

October 22

Insignificant

You don't like tea
or guns and sometimes
you don't like me.

We can always disagree
because we both know
we have humanity.

Friendship can see
any difference
no matter what it be.

And that is a beauty,
not insignificant,
to the likes of you and me.

October 23

Somebody Hurt You

Somebody hurt you,
but it wasn't me,
and I'm only trying to help,
can't you see?

Share your past
and the future is ours,
keep it locked up
and the past is who we are.

Somebody hurt you,
now you do the hurting,
and you always will
with those feelings you're skirting.

October 24

Door # 2

That's not what I expected
behind door number two,
but I am glad that I picked it,
the prize being you.

Of all life's choices,
and we have to make a few,
there's no doubt in my mind
you're the only choice that's true.

October 25

Bro Night

Boys will be boys,
but girls can't be girls
without the judgement
of the whole fucking world.
A night on the town
means two different things,
like a slap on the back
from the bros to the king,
but a slap to the face
of that bitch, that whore,
is a rite of passage
and a sign of what's in store.

October 26

Pivot

The goal,
the mission,
is straight ahead.
It seems so close,
within reach,
if you stay the course.
Then, life
throws obstacles
in your path,
but it's okay to pivot.
There are other ways
to travel instead.

October 27

DIY

Out of order,
all messed up,
broken,
beyond repair,
unfixable.

Some things are
if you don't have
the tools
and the know-how
to fix them.

October 28

We All Are

We all are racist,
prejudiced,
discriminatory,
and that will never change.

It's not a matter of race,
sex,
age,
but the fact that our eyes
can only see one thing.

Good thing our actions are malleable,
fluid,
righteous,
or else the world
would really be fucked.

October 29

Poor Yorick

After a while,
the meanings of words
become misconstrued,
altered by time
and culturally subdued.
Some phrases fall victim
to the backlash of hope
while others soar,
reaching outside
their menial scope.
Then there's the graveyard
where good verbiage
goes to die,
and like poor Yorick,
forever will they lie.

October 30

Whispers

The history lesson begins;
it's always the same.
Starts when the white man wins,
and takes away the red man's claim.
Millennia of stories lost,
snuffed out by greed.
Human lives the cost
of poorly sown seed.
Never written in ink,
but passed down by blood,
a never-ending link
to a time before the flood.
So old, so agèd, so wise,
so broken, so scattered,
and yet before our eyes
beautiful souls tattered.
Soldiers, carrying on.
Healers, soothing pain.
Protectors of tree and fawn
using nature, not for gain.

Of all the souls on earth,
they've changed and stayed the same.
True to the spirit's worth
and broken by the game.
Some stories have died,
never to be heard again,
and still their hearts are tried,
waiting for the moment when
culture and humanity clash
and history can be heard,
not written by those who were rash,
but spoken by those stirred
by a land,
that gave them life,
with a stand,
from years of strife.

A beauty, a persistence,
not set in stone,
a whisper of resistance,
echoed through the bone.

October 31

Basement Dive

Every basement has a ghost,
a monster,
hiding in the corners,
the creaks,
the pipes,
waiting for the lights
to go out
and for you to reach
the last step,
before safety,
before light,
and then,
he, she, it,

REACHES OUT,
grabs your ankle,
holds on tight,
and pulls you down
to…

November 1

Little Bird

With those winds whipping,
a little bird flaps twice as hard
when a safe haven
just isn't in the cards.

Who knows if she'll make it,
but she pushes with all her might,
even though she sees
not an end in sight.

She knows that if she stops,
her tired wings will fail,
so she's driven by the fact,
that one day she will sail.

November 2

Loathed

I am not meant
to nurture, to cultivate,
like those motherly types.

I am meant
to destroy, to deconstruct
in a few short swipes.

It's alright to be loathed
as long as you're good at it.

November 3

Digital Age

In this digital age
how is anyone supposed to know
how much I miss you
by looking at this photo?

My old crumpled favorites,
faded from age and sun,
kept close in my wallet
stuffed behind the ones
are visions made to move,
forever memorialized,
those I've lost,
burned into my eyes.

If anything good
is to come of this age,
I suppose your immortalization
is the work of a mage.

November 4

Pen Half-Dry

I like the pens you can see through;
they let you know where you stand.
You can see how much ink
you have left in your hand.

I can't say that I'm a pen half-full
or even a half-empty kind of gal,
but when the well has run dry,
it certainly affects the morale.

You can say there are other pens out there,
at least for the time being,
but when one ink won't match the other,
you'll find the words disagreeing.

November 5

Blood Junkie

It is cathartic,
at least to me,
not for helping others,
but for freeing me.
The needle in the flesh,
opening the vein,
is a bona fide rush;
I feel no pain.

Some seek a high,
by pushing poison in,
but I prefer losing
the blood beneath my skin.

November 6

Buried Alive

I'm that friend,
the one you lean on,
the shoulder to cry on,
the midnight call
that will always be answered,
the laughter in the tears,
and the saddest part is
all the weight I carry
is what is sure to bury
me alive
and there will be
no one to notice.

November 7

I Want You to Know Me

I want you
to know
that I think about you
all the time,
that my heart
races at the thought
of you, wanting
to know me.

November 8

Bless Your Heart

People don't understand the pain,
they think it is like stubbing a toe,
banging your head,
just some mundane feeling
fixed with drugs and bed.

If they ever really knew the
searing, excruciating, utterly unbearable feeling that rips you
apart from the inside out,

then maybe they
would have more to offer
than,
bless your heart.

November 9

313

There was cake;
that's all anyone
hopes for
at the bar.
Queens and pool,
fries and cake,
then pile
into the car.
We really knew
how to light up
the town.

November 10

Speaking Out

I know I am lucky
to have a mother
who taught me
to open my fuckin' mouth.
Not every little girl
gets that power
instilled in their bones.

I see these women,
so afraid to speak up,
speak out,
and I want to shake them,
rattle their souls.
Maybe I am part
of the ongoing problem,
encouraging weak ones
to be strong.
But this is me,
shaking you,
telling you,
to open
your fuckin' mouth.

November 11

DST

Saving time,
losing time,
eking out
or wishing away
those last few hours
of sun,
of light,
but all I know
is every hour
I am privileged to have,
belongs to you.

November 12

Spoiler Alert

There's this movie,
kind of popular,
maybe you've seen it?

It's about this guy
who goes into space,
ends up on a planet
where the human race
is almost extinct,
sold into slavery
by apes who took over
with undaunted bravery.

Spoiler alert:
here's where he was,
he landed on Earth
but in the future because
something about space
and time travel too,
but the point of the matter
is it could have been true.

The oppressed always rise
and the oppressor must fall,
and then it's the underdog
who takes over it all.
Just like the despot
they hoped to overtake,
then they take it too far
and build a new system to break.

November 13

Imago-ing

In transition
for seemingly
most of their lives,
until they flourish,
fluttering away
knowing they have
so few numbered days.
Beauty and pollen,
the songbird
sweetly sings.
Regret is never carried
on the butterfly's wings.

November 14

Certainty

He wasn't ready,
but who is?
Shocking, since
it's one of life's certainties.
From day one,
the first breath
in our lungs,
we know it will end.
We may not know
the where or the when,
the how or the why.
Life should have prepared him
for the day he would die.

November 15

Goals

My aspirations have never strayed farther
than just living,
so I suppose I've been content.

I need nothing more
than air to breathe
and a mild promise
that tomorrow I will wake.

If that promise should fall apart,
I'll die having reached my goals
and there's no better point to life
than filling up your soul.

November 16

Don't Stop Believing

When did you stop believing,
or do you still think
there's a man in a red suit
that can traverse the world in a blink?
I guess it's no more farfetched
than the parting of the sea
or a resurrection scheduled
for the salvation of you or me.
Fairy tales serve a purpose
to keep you in your place
and blind your starry eyes
better than a can of mace.

November 17

Misplaced Luggage

Who cares where you've been?
You probably don't want to know
all about my past.
I could fill a luggage set
with all the promises
I had hoped would last.
Let's just pack our bags,
check them at the terminal,
and make a break fast.
We can tell those handlers
to misplace our battered baggage
and we can move on at last.

November 18

Sex

Sex sells, kills, creates,
a biological imperative
we are unable to sedate.
Do you, you know,
on the first date?
Let's not talk about
the fact that you're late
or the test results
on which you wait.
Let's not talk at all,
no feelings to state,
pretend we don't care,
don't take the bait,
just light 'em up
and say, "hey, that was great."

November 19

Dirty Snowbanks

A smooth blanket
of white packed snow,
lacking imperfection
as the piles grow
looks beautiful,
we all know.

Beauty is oft missed
in those roadside crusts
of dirt and salt
that the plow had thrust
away to the side
because they must.

Like all in life,
both will not last,
and the awe and ugliness
will be in the past
until the next time
snow is forecast.

November 20

Self-Help

It is a wonder to think
that some folks have
the time & money
to have problems.
They can buy the books,
watch the videos,
pay the therapist
to fix the problems
that they've created
themselves.
All that self-centered bullshit
and those enlightened ways of thinking,
it don't pay the rent
nor keep the lights on.

November 21

Crafty Woman

Can you imagine
an imagination so grand
to run away
with only hope at hand?
An oppressive era in time,
yes more so than today,
a woman posed as a man
in order to get away.
Despite her fairer skin,
there was nothing fair about being Black
and with her husband's help,
they fought the odds, fully stacked.
All those simple fuckers,
who thought that slavery was right,
had no clue this man before them
was a woman who was not white.

November 22

Tying the Knot

A nice square knot
for tying two together,
secure and stable,
like it could last forever.

A clove hitch
is easy to tie,
but quick to come apart
with any little lie.

A blood knot
can mend a broken line;
severed ends exposed
is never a good sign.

The hangman's knot,
even when tied loosely,
tightens quickly with
every *sorry* spilled profusely.

November 23

Better

I don't think it gets better
unless you make it be better;
you can't really wait
for change to spontaneously combust
and set fire to evil,
despots, drudgery, and
just plain cloudy days.
It doesn't get better,
you do.

November 24

Watermelon

Faded into the background,
the extras play their parts,
mumbling on in silence
as the leads poured out their hearts.
No one gives a thought
to those walking shadows,
strutting, fretting,
concealing all their woes.
Their mouths are always moving,
but no one hears a thing.
Their lives remain mysteries,
waiting in the wings.

November 25

TXT

Hey

                                      Yo

Hows ur day?

                                      oh, u know

that bad?

                                      in so many ways

can I help?

                                      u already did

☺

                                      my feelings exactly

November 26

Retail

The title says it all
to make this some nasty verse.
Anyone who has worked it
knows its evil curse.
Ungrateful bastards
berate you all day long
as the soul is destroyed,
no matter if you are strong.
Just extend your wrists
and open the vein,
it's a more pleasant experience
than working for the insane.

November 27

Laissez Faire

A certain je ne sais quoi
about the Big Easy
makes sure that life
is light and breezy.
The people, the music,
the culture, the food,
all make it hard for even
the darkest heart to brood.

How you doing?
Where you from?
Everyone comes together,
each totaling the sum.
The city never sleeps,
its heart forever beats
to the sound of the drums
playing in the streets.

November 28

Cross Words

D	A	M	N					L						
		A						E						
I	N	D	I	G	N	A	N	T						
								D		M				
								O		I				
								W		S				
		S	H	A	M	E	O	N	Y	O	U			
										N				
										D				
									V	E	X	E	D	
										R				
										S				
										T	E	P	I	D
										O				
										O				
D	I	S	A	P	P	O	I	N	T	E	D			

November 29

Warm Bodies

Let the snowbanks grow,
we've nowhere to go,
and the firewood's stacked,
not a thing is lacked.
Should the power go out,
I have not a doubt
we could find a way
to keep the cold at bay.

November 30

Breaking Glass

Breaking glass
is a messy task,
and even more so
when you're done,
since you've got
to pick it all up,
and hope not to cut
anyone.

December 1

ISO

In search of something,
something unknown,
unknown to the mind,
mindful to the soul.
Soul-searching,
searching the stars,
starry eyes,
eyes on the prize.

December 2

Vegetative State

Hooked to the screens,
life support
for a brain
no longer firing.
Blank stares
and muscle memory,
quickly fading,
constantly tiring.
A generation
out of touch,
lost in tech,
a vegetative state.
Pull the plug,
drift away,
power down,
a blank slate.

December 3

Board Meeting

Fresh powder
on the first run
and a flash of pink
cuts in front of the sun.
Each trip down,
the slopes gain a crowd,
but my eyes still catch
you skimming the clouds.
Rosy cheeks and lighting
as night settles in;
the crowds have dispersed,
the lift on the last spin.
Watching you move
has warmed me all day,
but sharing this chair
will keep us warm until May.

December 4

Shortstop

It was always a dream
to play shortstop
on Turner Field.

Dreams die
far too quickly
when you find out
your tits exclude you
from playing ball.

December 5

Country Night

The city lights
sure can be pretty,
but they got nothing
on the sky outside the city.
A country night,
with crisper air,
brilliant stars,
and not a single care.

December 6

Improv

Every day is a new scene,
dialogue, interactions, chuckles,
and every word is
a constant struggle.
All an act,
just to force a smile.
At least *you'll* be laughing
for a little while.

December 7

Monster under the Bed

Have you ever had the feeling
there's a monster under your bed,
or those red eyes in the closet
that fill your being with dread?
Did you ever ask one question
that would put your heart at ease
and find a way to correct
the brisk and bumpy seas?
All those creatures that you fear
could be trembling on their own
and hiding out from you
in a world all alone.

December 8

Hole in the Wall

Yell at me again,
how else will I know
you love me?

Put a hole in the wall,
spew the venom,
help me see

just how hard it is
to be you.
No fists are needed,
words will do.

December 9

The Cure

Heart racing,
breath catching,
weak knees,
this is the end
for sure.
Those eyes,
that dress,
your smile,
you're my ailment
and my cure.

December 10

Straight Girl, Crushed

It never ends well,
loving someone
who can't love you back,
but that never stops
the hope, the endless,
subtle pursuit
of inevitable heartbreak.

December 11

Self-Love

I thought, one time,
falling in love
would be divine,
but quickly changed
my budding mind,
listened to my heart,
and the signs,
to find that love of self
is perfectly fine.

December 12

She Loves Me: Reprise

Most of the petals
have fallen away
and a withering flower,
won't make it but a day,
She loves me,
she loves me not,
are vacant
and distant thoughts,
decomposing
before my very eyes,
beauty always fades
before it dies.

December 13

I Don't

I don't need the movie scenes,
all Hollywood,
plastic and fake.
I don't need the romantic dreams,
turning to nightmares,
all full of snakes.
I don't need the love song,
professing,
possessing,
the pulsing of hearts.
I don't need a ring,
shining,
sparkling,
threatening to tear us apart.
I just want you,
exactly as you are,
filled with fault
and showing scars.

December 14

La nieve

Nevó ayer
y pensé en ti,
cómo fuimos a la deriva
como esos copos de nieve.

La próxima vez
que piense en ti,
espero que la lluvia
se lleve la memoria.

Snow

It snowed yesterday
and I thought of you,
how we drifted apart,
like snowflakes do.

The next time
that I think of you,
I hope that the rain
will wash the memory away too.

December 15

Profit and Loss

The things we lose,
our innocence,
our virginity,
our minds,
are such minor dues to pay
for all the things we gain:
clarity,
pleasure,
freedom.

December 16

Beamish Boy

Fuckin' Jabberwock
and frumious Bandersnatch!
All they had to do
was stay alive
just long enough
to ensure
that the real monster
fell on his own
vorpal blade.

December 17

Songbird

Jubilant chirps
from creatures so small
mean new life
is starting to crawl.
All that withered away
when the leaves started to fall,
will unfurl its wings
and gently enthrall
the world at large
with an elegant call
that is heard by one,
but meant for all.

December 18

Eightball

One part gamble,
two parts skill,
clearing the table,
going in for the kill,
sinking your teeth,
drinking your fill,
damning your soul,
downing the pill,
snorting the coke,
to sedate the will.

December 19

Indy & Lara

Foolish kids,
running up and down the aisles.
Making a movie,
making a memory,
one of many.
A zombie around every corner,
a B movie masterpiece
just waiting
for the cutting room floor.
What a bust.
But one day,
the zombies will be us,
limping through the aisles,
still making memories.

December 20

Huddled Masses

Together,
hoping for a better life,
these monsters at the gate,
filled with longing and strife
await a time
when their voices will be heard,
carried on the winds
to the corrupt and absurd
if only to open
the gates and the eyes
of those who wear humanity
as a frivolous disguise.

December 21

Sweet Diversity

This fight is nothing new.
It's carried on for years
and it's never gonna' end
'til we realize that deep inside,
we're truly all the same.

They tell us what to do
and how to fit in their little box.
So scared they'll lose control,
or worse, they'll be exposed
as the tyrants that they are.

Our differences make us great.
Who knows if they'll ever see
that the world is built on change
and continues to grow strong
with our sweet diversity?

December 22

Lone Wolf

A lone wolf
and a cold moon,
chill sets in
with impending gloom.
Lost on a mountain
on a wintery night
with no fire
for warmth or light.
Survival or doom,
which card to pull,
choices to make,
decisions to mull.
Climb down the trail
or stay where you are,
but another lone wolf
will never be far.

December 23

The Wait

The excitement is overwhelming,
the anticipation, unbearable,
like unwrapping a present
although not really comparable.
More like a night
full of tosses and turns,
or waiting for the fire
to catch and brightly burn.
The nerves tingling on edge,
the breath, caught in your throat,
the veins teeming with hope
in every word I wrote.

December 24

Ironic?

I tried to write a poem
all about irony,
but failed from the start,
verses unable to agree.

A rhyme scheme here
and a quatrain there,
but the prose fell flat;
the poet didn't care.

What a poem this is,
how perfectly it rhymes,
the beauty of the language
is apparent.

December 25

Delusional

I'm not delusional,
I am well aware
that world peace
is a pipe dream.

It's the little things,
acts of kindness,
selfless deeds that
make it better than it seems.

I know greed,
I know human nature,
I know love, and
I know hate.

And, while the world burns,
it's no illusion,
the magic of humanity
and the will to create.

December 26

Soon

Eventually,
I'll fix that leak,
I'll get to
that stack of books,
the next ball game,
I'll attend.

Someday,
I'll take that class,
learn that language,
visit that island,
see that view.

Soon,
it'll be too late
and all that's left
is a list of to-dos.

December 27

Feeling Mortal

Youth feels like
immortality,
untouchable, unreachable,
utterly free.

Age brings wisdom
and mortality,
but I wouldn't trade it for youthful days
filled with uncertainty.

December 28

A Dime A Dozen Disease

Eking out an existence
is never anyone's dream,
in fact it's been known
to make a few lost souls scream.
Poverty, a dime a dozen disease,
spread by the wealthy with ease.
Existing on the fringes,
always viewed, but never seen,
just some more souls
lost in the machine.
The true minority, doing as they please
while the rest of us struggle and wheeze.

December 29

ov e k'imy

Adventurer,
intellectual,
pun-maker
extraordinaire.

Thrill-seeker,
couch surfer,
food explorer
at the fair.

Music lover,
trivia maven,
animal rescuer
with flair.

Good friend,
smile maker,
laugh creator,
a gem so rare.

December 30

Tolerate

Tolerate,
it's really a nasty word
when you think about it.
The definition
insinuates
something is wrong
with you,
your way of life,
your beliefs.
It encourages others to
discriminate,
not to accept,
but to point out
differences
that only ignorance
can create.

December 31

the day before

the city does sleep, and that's my favorite time to meander the maze of empty streets before the sweeps clean the grime of the day before since every life worth living is like those quiet, littered streets:

shaped,
altered,
changed,
by the events
of the day before

The following Leap Day poem was written by Emilita Isabella María Santina Anna Pinta Guadalupe Dominga Rodríguez Sanchez Scroogè Siders de las Botas

February 26

Leap

Doing the math,
judging the distance,
figuring out
the path of least resistance.

A towering height
for a creature so small,
and if I jump,
there's a chance I could fall.

But chances are fleeting,
decisions must be made,
and chances not taken
cause opportunities to fade.

So, what will it be?
What reward will I reap?
The only way to know
is to take that leap.

Acknowledgements

I'll never tire of thanking Kerry Swain, and I hope she never tires of turning my ideas into art. Thanks for having me covered!

Brittney Six, thanks for giving me inspiration when the well started to dry. You're the only person who will text back at midnight, and while you may not appreciate that, I do.

Many thanks to Emilita for providing a poem for leap day. I know your days are filled with naps and I greatly appreciate your contribution. You are my everything.

To Me, I never have to question whether you love me or not. You deal with my range of emotions on a daily basis, but never give up on me. I love you forever.

For Inquiring Minds
(all the songs used in "Title")

Cline, Patsy. "Crazy." *Showcase*. Decca, 1961.

Carter, Deana. "Strawberry Wine." *Did I Shave My Legs for This?* Capitol and Nashville, 1995.

Jackson, Alan. "Chattahoochee." *A Lot About Livin' (And a Little 'bout Love)*. Arista, 1992.

Beethoven, Ludwig van, composer. "Moonlight Sonata." Op. 27, No. 2. 1801.

McBryde, Ashley. "Never Will." *Never Will*. Warner Music and Nashville, 2020.

Fitzgerald, Ella, and Count Basie Orchestra. "Them There Eyes." *Ella and Basie!* Verve, 1963.

The Quintet. "A Night in Tunisia." *Jazz at Massey Hall*. Debut/OJC America, 1953.

Fleetwood Mac. "Songbird." *Rumours*. Warner Bros., 1977.

No Doubt. "Spiderwebs." *Tragic Kingdom*. Trauma and Interscope, 1995.

Branch, Michelle. "Drop in the Ocean." *The Spirit Room*. Maverick and Warner Bros., 2001.

Bareilles, Sara. "She Used to Be Mine." *What's Inside: Songs from Waitress*. Epic, 2015.

Hozier. "In a Week." *Hozier*. Rubyworks, Island, and Columbia, 2014.

Barenaked Ladies. "One Week." *Stunt*. Reprise, 1998.

38 Special. "Caught Up in You." *Special Forces*. A&M, 1982.

The Who. "Behind Blue Eyes." *Who's Next*. Track and Decca, 1971.

Fleetwood Mac. "Gypsy." *Mirage*. Warner Bros., 1982.

Santana, Carlos and Thomas. "Smooth." *Supernatural*. Arista, 1999.

Fleetwood Mac. "Gold Dust Woman." *Rumours*. Warner Bros., 1977.

Red Hot Chili Peppers. "Otherside." *Californication*. Warner Bros., 1999.

Berigan, Bunny. "I Can't Get Started." *A Symposium of Swing*. Victor, 1943.

McBryde, Ashley. "A Little Dive Bar in Dahlonega." *Girl Going Nowhere*. Warner Bros. and Nashville, 2018.

Latifah, Queen. "I Know Where I've Been." *Hairspray Soundtrack*. New Line, 2007.

Cohn, Marc. "Walking in Memphis." *Marc Cohn*. Atlantic, 1991.

Pentatonix. "Light in the Hallway." *Pentatonix*. RCA, 2015.

Pentatonix. "Take Me Home." *Pentatonix*. RCA, 2015.

P!nk. "Beautiful Trauma." *Beautiful Trauma*. RCA, 2017.

About the Authors

Autumn Siders lives in New Hampshire with the world-famous cat, Emilita. She holds a B.A. in English from the University of New Hampshire and manages The Country Bookseller in Wolfeboro. She is the author of *#nofilter*, *Not My Type: Stories,* and *Spermeo & Juliegg: A Reproductive Tragedy.* She also maintains the blog, butwiththemind.com.

Emilita Isabella María Santina Anna Pinta Guadalupe Dominga Rodríguez Sanchez Scroogè Siders de las Botas grew up in the mean shelters of the Lakes Region of New Hampshire. As soon as she found two schmucks who would fall for her act, she made her furever home with them. Her work has been the focal point of *#nofilter, Not My Type: Stories, Spermeo & Juliegg: A Reproductive Tragedy,* and the blog butwiththemind.com. When she is not writing, she cannot be found unless she is sleeping or eating.

www.ingramcontent.com/pod-product-compliance
Lightning Source LLC
Chambersburg PA
CBHW020859080526
44589CB00011B/365